COMPUTER MODELS IN FINANCE
SOFTWARE FOR FINANCIAL MANAGEMENT

LAWRENCE E. McLEAN
Fayetteville State University
Fayetteville, NC

Macmillan Publishing Company
New York

Maxwell Macmillan Canada
Toronto

Maxwell Macmillan International
New York Oxford Singapore Sydney

> IMPORTANT NOTICE REGARDING SOFTWARE WARRANTY DISCLAIMER
> AND LIMITATION OF LIABILITIES
>
> Macmillan Publishing Company and the author **do not** warrant that the Computer Models in Finance software package will function properly in every hardware/software environment.
>
> Macmillan Publishing Company and the author of this software exclude any and all implied warranties, including warranties of merchantability and fitness for a particular purpose, and limit your remedy to return of the software to Macmillan Publishing Company for replacement.
>
> Although this software has been tested and the documentation reviewed, Macmillan Publishing Company and the author make no warranty or representation, either express or implied, with respect to this software or documentation, their quality, performance, merchantability, or fitness for a particular purpose. This software and documentation are provided "as is" and the user is assuming the entire risk as to their quality and performance.
>
> In no event will Macmillan Publishing Company or the author be liable for direct, indirect, special, incidental or consequential damages arising out of the use or inability to use the software or documentation.
>
> The warranty and remedies set forth above are exclusive and in lieu of all others, oral or written, express or implied.

Copyright © 1994 by Macmillan Publishing Company, a division of Macmillan, Inc.

Printed in the United States of America

All rights reserved. No part of this book may be reproduced or
transmitted in any form or by any means, electronic or mechanical,
including photocopying, recording, or any information storage and
retrieval system, without permission in writing from the publisher.

Macmillan Publishing Company
866 Third Avenue, New York, New York 10022

Macmillan Publishing Company is part
of the Maxwell Communication Group of Companies.

Maxwell Macmillan Canada, Inc.
1200 Eglinton Avenue East
Suite 200
Don Mills, Ontario M3C 3N1

ISBN 0-02-379391-0

Printing: 1 2 3 4 5 6 7 8   Year: 4 5 6 7 8 9 0 1 2 3

CONTENTS

CHAPTER		PAGE
	PREFACE	v
	PART I: INTRODUCTION	1
1	Getting Started	3
2	Computer Basics	13
3	How to Use CMF	15
	PART II: TIME VALUE OF MONEY	27
4	Present and Future Value	29
5	Annuities	33
6	Perpetuities	35
7	Time Value Tables	39
8	Compounding Frequency	41
	PART III: RISK AND RETURN	43
9	Stock Risk and Return	45
10	Portfolio Risk and Return	49
	PART IV: VALUATION	53
11	Bonds	55
12	Mortgages	59
13	Leases	65
14	Preferred Stock	67
15	Common Stock	69

CHAPTER		PAGE
	PART V: STATEMENT ANALYSIS	73
16	Overview of Financial Statements	75
17	Financial Statements	79
18	Ratio Analysis	89
19	Common Size Analysis	93
20	Changes in Financial Position	97
21	Pro Forma Statements	99
	PART VI: FORECASTING	115
22	Cash Budgeting	117
23	Sustainable Growth	127
	PART VII: CAPITAL BUDGETING	131
24	Capital Budgeting	133
25	Lease-Buy Analysis	145
	PART VIII: FINANCING	149
26	Cost of Capital	151
27	Leverage	153
	PART IX: WORKING CAPITAL	159
28	EOQ Inventory Model	161
29	Cash Balances	163

PREFACE

Computer Models in Finance (CMF) consists of 25 financial models designed to solve common financial problems. CMF is not meant to be used as a financial text but as a supplement to financial management texts. By providing easy-to-use software designed to solve a broad range of financial problems, CMF strives to ease the calculation effort associated with undergraduate and MBA courses in finance.

Models pertaining to the following topics are provided:

TIME VALUE OF MONEY	FORECASTING
RISK AND RETURN	CAPITAL BUDGETING
VALUATION	FINANCING
STATEMENT ANALYSIS	WORKING CAPITAL

The software is written for the Lotus 1-2-3 version 2.X. (Certain socalled "1-2-3 compatible" software may also run the CMF templates. Please refer to the section on "Quattro and other compatible software" in Chapter 1 for some relevant comments regarding compatibility.) An IBM PC or compatible capable of running 1-2-3 is necessary.

Lotus 1-2-3 is the preferred choice of financial practitioners because of its ease of use, wide-ranging capabilities and its ability to perform sensitivity analysis. The selection of a spreadsheet rather than Basic, Fortran, Pascal or other highlevel languages was based upon a belief by the author that such a choice is more relevant for students. There is a very small probability that students, once outside the academic world, will ever program with high-level languages. On the other hand, if they are to practice finance (or any other business discipline, for that matter), it is virtually certain they will use spreadsheets.

CMF models differ from other competing financial-based software in several ways:

1. The models are not tied to a particular textbook but are designed so that they can be used with any finance text or set of cases.

2. The models are not tied to specific problems. They are designed to handle classes of problems such as time value of money, capital budgeting, etc. The robustness of the models enables them to solve broad ranges of financial problems.

3. No prior computer knowledge is assumed or required of either the instructor or the students.

4. No computer programming or teaching of 1-2-3 is required. Virtually all course and homework time devoted to the use of CMF will be time devoted to finance.

5. The models are completely menu-driven.

6. All models have the same easy-to-use menu interface. From a user standpoint, knowing how to use one model is equivalent to knowing how to use them all (except for the financial knowledge required).

7. The models ar not limited to textbook applications but can be utilized in real-world business settings.

If you require technical support, please feel free to fax the author c/o PFS at (911) 295•3390.

IMPORTANCE OF TEXT IN THE BUSINESS AND CLASSROOM ENVIRONMENTS:

1. The business community has accepted the microcomputer and continues to integrate it as a decision-support tool. University placement personnel are discovering that microcomputer skills are becoming an important attribute in securing employment. This fact is reflected in the American Assembly of Collegiate Schools of Business accreditation activities where member schools are being required to document the nature and extent of microcomputer applications in the curriculum.

2. Computer skill level is used by some businesses as a proxy measure to judge the quality of education. Lack of microcomputer familiarity and application skills puts students at a disadvantage in the marketplace.

3. Financial applications have led other functional business areas. Financial forecasting, analysis and planning have been automated on mainframe computers for many years. Microcomputers and spreadsheets have enabled these functions to be shifted to the desk of the financial manager/analyst where more timely and relevant information can be obtained.

4. Finance courses are under pressure to include more subjects in the same time allotment. The finance professor does not have the time (and often not the experience) to include instruction concerning the use of financial spreadsheets in the curriculum. CMF provides spreadsheet capability with a minimum of spreadsheet instruction.

5. The teaching of finance involves a tradeoff between concepts and applications. The tedious and time-consuming nature of applications. when done by hand, severely limits this aspect of teaching. The availability of financial models enables a substantial increase in the applications work without a commensurate increase in student time-commitment. CMF eliminates this time consuming and tedious element from the finance course.

6. Increased use of applications reinforces the understanding of concepts. Use of the computer prepares the student in the "how to" aspects of finance, an important consideration for acceptable performance in the business community. Familiarity with financial spreadsheet analysis produces benefits in non-finance courses where financial techniques are required (e.g. Business Policy) and encourages student-driven applications that go beyond finance.

IMPORTANT FEATURES OF THE TEXT

Computer Models in Finance is not a programming book. Financial problem-solving using software models is the emphasis. Some of the important features of the text are the following:

* Ease of use. The software is menu-driven enabling the novice to easily move from model to model. A common menu interface is used for all models.

* Help screens are available should they be necessary.

* All models are accompanied by representative problems with step-by- step, illustrative solutions provided.

* "Sensitivity analysis" is emphasized in order to demonstrate the relative importance of variables in financial decision models.

* Software graphics, where applicable, are available as a pedagogical and analytical assist.

* Calculation effort is dramatically reduced from calculator or pencil-based solutions.

* The text is cross-referenced to leading finance texts.

COMPUTER SKILLS

Comptuer knowledge or programming skill is not required of either the professor or the student to use CMF; neither does CMF teach it. Instructors and students ignorant of computers may retain this blissful condition, if so desired, and still successfully use CMF. (Such a blissful condition is, however, not optimal for future business success.) A major advantage of this book is that it does not divert already strained class time from finance to computer instruction. The easy-to-solve problems provide a valuable pedagogical assist which enables more in-depth treatment of topics than is presently afforded in the standard finance course.

ADVANTAGES OF MODELING

The use of the computer-assisted financial models provides advantages to both teacher and student. The author believes that the following benefits occur when microcomputer modeling is utilized in finance classes:

* Understanding of important concepts such as the time value of money, cash flows, risk and sensitivity analysis is increased.

* Problem-solving in finance becomes more tractable.

* Student calculation time is decreased.

* Spreadsheet familiarity and proficiency encourages computer applications in other business courses.

* The perceived value of the finance course is enhanced in the eyes of both students and businesssmen.

* Students enjoy the use of computers to solve problems that previously were considered tedious and time-consuming.

* The software can be integrated into lectures where virtually instantaneous sensitivity analysis and graphics can be used by the instructor to highlight issues.

While the use of CMF templates can complement the financial learning process, the templates are no substitute for proper study habits. They will undoubtedly reduce some of the "drudgery" associated with number crunching. Hopefully, they will also provide better proficiency in the "how to" aspects of financial management as well as better conceptual understanding of the underlying fundamentals of finance.

PART I:
INTRODUCTION

		PAGE
Chapter 1:	Getting Started	5
Chapter 2:	Computer Basics	15
Chapter 3:	How to Use CMF	19

The three chapters in Part I are introductory. They supply the basic information necessary to use the <u>Computer Models in Finance</u> (CMF) models. No models are presented in this first section of the book. A brief summary of the chapters is provided below.

<u>Chapter 1</u>: should be read prior to using the software.

<u>Chapter 2</u>: may be skipped by those familiar with computers, diskettes and the MS DOS operating system.

<u>Chapter 3</u>: is a reference chapter for the CMF software. It is recommended that users read it prior to using the software. It is a chapter that most users will refer back to if questions arise.

On page 3 is a table of contents for Part I of this book. Because Part I will be used mostly as a reference, it was deemed necessary to include such a table to facilitate finding subjects of interest. This table of contents can be very useful when referring back to any of the first three chapters in this book.

Chapter 1 GETTING STARTED

SUMMARY
This chapter provides an overview of <u>Computer Models in Finance</u> (CMF). This overview includes a brief review of the software models, suggestions on how to use this book and how to get a "quick start" using CMF.

WHAT DO YOU NEED IN ADDITION TO CMF
To use the CMF software you will need the following:

1. Lotus 1-2-3 (versions 2.X are supported). Other software that may run CMF is discussed below under the section "QUATTRO AND OTHER COMPATIBLE SOFTWARE."

2. An IBM PC (or its equivalent). The original PC (Intel 8088 chip), AT, 386 and 486's are supported. (The forthcoming Pentium chip should also work.)

3. A 3.5 inch floppy disk is required. (A hard disk is not necessary but useful.)

QUATTRO AND OTHER COMPATIBLE SOFTWARE
Several competing spreadsheet products may be satisfactory for running CMF. The key to compatibility is whether the competing software uses the Lotus 1-2-3 menu structure. This is important because the 1-2-3 menu structure is used in the macros that drive the CMF software.

IT IS THE USER'S RESPONSIBILITY TO VERIFY COMPATIBILITY OF COMPETING SOFTWARE. THE PUBLISHER CANNOT TEST ALL SOFTWARE AND HARDWARE COMBINATIONS.

The following comments are believed to be correct but <u>**should be verified by the user**</u> prior to committing to the CMF software:

Quattro
Many versions of Borland's Quattro are able to run CMF. Early versions of Quattro are compatible but the newest versions may not be. Recently, Lotus was able to prevent Borland from providing the 1-2-3 menu option in its software. Versions of Quattro that have the Lotus menu option appear to run CMF without problem. This includes all versions of Quattro through the first versions of Quattro Pro 4.0 (later releases of Quattro Pro version 4 may not provide this option). Quattro Pro for Windows does not have menu compatibility and hence cannot be used to run CMF. If you wish to use Quattro to run CMF, you must run Quattro with the 1-2-3 menu option activated (i.e. in Lotus 1-2-3 menu mode).

Lotus 1-2-3 for Windows and Lotus 1-2-3 version 3.X
It is believed, but has not been verified, that all higher numbered versions of Lotus are downward compatible with Lotus 2.X.

Other Products
There is other software that purports to be Lotus 1-2-3 compatible. VP Planner and As Easy As 123 are two such products. A source for VP Planner is not known. As Easy As 123 is a shareware product which can be obtained via BBS downloading or from companies that distribute shareware for a nominal price (generally about $5.00). However, usage of shareware generally obligates the user to a relatively low payment to the developer in order to continue using the product. Both of these products are believed to be compatible with Lotus 2.1 and able to run CMF.

Other products, from time to time, have claimed compatibility with Lotus 1-2-3. Two examples are Lucid and Supercalc. The author cannot comment on their ability to run CMF.

REVIEW OF THE MODELS
<u>Computer Models in Finance</u> (CMF) is a collection of 25 models or templates designed to solve various problems in finance. (It should be noted that the terms "model" and "template" will be used interchangeably throughout the book.) CMF deals with the following subjects:

TIME VALUE OF MONEY	FORECASTING
RISK AND RETURN	CAPITAL BUDGETING
VALUATION	FINANCING
STATEMENT ANALYSIS	WORKING CAPITAL

Each of these topics represents a separate section in this book and consists of two or more models. Each model is represented by a chapter (see Table of Contents on page ix) which explains the purpose of the model, how to use it and any limitations that may apply.

The models, grouped by topic, and their software names are shown in Exhibit I-1 on the following page. The number in parenthesis after the topic is the number of models pertaining to that section. The software name is the file name used to store the file on diskette (see chapter 3 for directly accessing files via these filenames). Note that PLAN and LEASEBUY appear twice. They are the same models, but may be accessed from two different software menus. (The chapter write-ups of these two models occur in the topic grouping where the models are listed without brackets.)

EXHIBIT I-1

DESCRIPTION	SOFTWARE NAME
TIME VALUE OF MONEY (5)	
Present and Future Value	TIMEVAL
Annuities	ANNUITY
Perpetuities	PERPETUY
Time Value Tables	TABLE
Compounding Frequency	COMPFREQ
RISK AND RETURN (2)	
Stock Risk and Return	BETA
Portfolio Risk and Return	PORT
VALUATION (5)	
Bonds	BOND
Mortgages	MORT
Leases	LEASE
Preferred Stock	PREFER
Common Stock	STOCK
STATEMENT ANALYSIS (5)	
Financial Statements	FINSTATE
Ratio Analysis	RATIO
Common Size Analysis	COMSIZE
Changes in Fin'l Position	FUNDSFLO
Pro Forma Statements	PLAN
FORECASTING (3)	
Cash Budgeting	CASHBUD
[Pro Forma Statements	PLAN]
Sustainable Growth	GROWTH
CAPITAL BUDGETING (2)	
Capital Budgeting	CAPBUD
Lease-Buy Analysis	LEASEBUY
FINANCING (3)	
Cost of Capital	COSTCAP
[Lease-Buy Analysis	LEASEBUY]
Leverage	LEVERAGE
WORKING CAPITAL (2)	
EOQ Inventory Model	EOQ
Cash Balances	CASHBAL

SUGGESTED GUIDE AS TO HOW TO USE THIS BOOK
The purpose of this book is to assist you in using the CMF models. The manner in which the book is used depends upon an individual's experience with computers and the manner in which he/she best learns.

The author offers the following suggestions regarding the learning of CMF via the use of this book.

1. Read Chapter 1 (this chapter).

2. Read Chapter 2 if you are a computer novice (see below to determine whether you are or are not a novice), or need a refresher on computer basics

3. Read Chapter 3. Do not try to learn this chapter on first reading. Have it handy for reference when you use the software. This chapter has been designed primarily as a reference chapter to answer general questions regarding CMF. It is the chapter you will probably use most frequently.

4. Read carefully the CMF chapter pertaining to a particular model prior to using it. Make sure you also understand the underlying financial theory as explained in your textbook. Work the illustrative problem(s) provided to gain confidence and to ensure that you understand how to use the model.

AM I A COMPUTER NOVICE (SHOULD I READ CHAPTER 2)?
It may be possible to skip chapter 2 in your reading of this manual. If you know how to use an IBM PC (or compatible) and have used Lotus 1-2-3 before, you probably do not have to read Chapter 2. If you are unsure whether you possess the basic skills required, how you answer the following four questions will tell you whether you should read Chapter 2:

1. Have you used floppy diskettes before?

2. Do you know how to "boot-up" an IBM PC (including the entering of the time and date)?

3. Do you know how to make "back-up" copies of diskettes?

4. Do you know how to load Lotus 1-2-3?

If you answered any of the above questions "NO," then you should read Chapter 2 prior to using the software. Even if you answered them all "YES" you may wish to read chapter 2 (although it probably will repeat information that you have already acquired).

THE FIRST STEP -- MAKE A BACK-UP OF THE CMF SOFTWARE
It is assumed that you know how to properly handle and copy diskettes. If this assumption is incorrect, stop reading this chapter and go to Chapter 2 (or consult your MS DOS manual or your computer operating manual). Chapter 2 provides the directions necessary to back-up the CMF software diskette.

Prior to proceeding any further:

MAKE A BACK-UP COPY OF THE CMF DISKETTE !!!

Store the original in a safe place.
Use only the back-up copy.

THE SECOND STEP -- CONFIGURE THE SOFTWARE FOR YOUR COMPUTER
Most users have computers with one floppy disk drive and a hard disk. The software may be run from either the floppy or the hard drive.

To run CMF from the floppy, skip to the next section which deals with "A Quick Start With CMF." If you have a hard-disk machine and would like to run the software from the hard-disk, refer to "Installing the CMF Software" in Chapter 2.

A QUICK START WITH CMF
This section is meant to be used only by those **readers who are computer literate** and have a working **knowledge of Lotus 1-2-3**. It provides a guide for using the software immediately. Even for these users, however, **it is suggested that Chapter 3 be read prior to using the software** and that this manual be kept nearby for reference should it be required. Remember: when in doubt, consult this manual.

Prior to proceeding:

Make sure that software is backed-up and that it has been configured properly for your computer.

The following steps are your guide to a quick start with CMF:

1. Boot up Lotus 1-2-3.

2. Place the <u>backed-up</u> (never use your original) CMF diskette into the disk drive. Change the 1-2-3 default drive to the directory that contains the CMF diskette. To change the default drive to drive A, for example, type **/FDA:<RET>** where "/FD" is the file directory command; "A:" changes to the A directory or drive where the CMF software is; and "<RET>" signifies that you should press the ENTER KEY (i.e. do not type).

3. Type **/FR FINANCE<RET>** where "/FR" is the file retrieve command from Lotus; "FINANCE" is the name of the file you are to retrieve; and "<RET>" signifies that you should press the ENTER KEY (i.e. do not type). (Chapter 3 has a detailed description of the keys and nomenclature used in this manual.) You will see the title screen shown as Exhibit I-2.

EXHIBIT I-2

CMF TITLE SCREEN

(FACSIMILE OF THE COMPUTER MONITOR)

```
================================================================
$\                    COMPUTER MODELS IN FINANCE              /$
$$$\                  ==============================          /$$$
$$$$$\                  A Series of Templates                 /$$$$$
$$$$$$$\                   Designed to Solve                  /$$$$$$$
$$$$$$$$$\            Financial Management Problems           /$$$$$$$$$
$$$$$$$$$$$                                                   $$$$$$$$$$$
$$$$$$$$$/                     developed by                   \$$$$$$$$$
$$$$$$$/               Lawrence E. McLean, PhD                \$$$$$$$
$$$$$/                                                        \$$$$$
$$$/                   Fayetteville State University          \$$$
$/                          Fayetteville, NC                  \$
================================================================
================================================================
            Copyright (C) by Macmillan Publishing Company, 1994

                              CMF 2.00
================================================================
                   Press <RET> to go to MAIN MENU
================================================================
```

4. Press <RET> to move to the MAIN MENU which appears as Exhibit I-3 below.

EXHIBIT I-3

CMF MAIN MENU

(FACSIMILE OF THE COMPUTER MONITOR)

```
================================================================
                            MAIN MENU
================================================================
     Number     Category                                  Number
     ----------------------------------------------------------
       - 1    TIME VALUE OF MONEY    ------------------     1
       - 2    RISK AND RETURN        ------------------     2
       - 3    VALUATION              ------------------     3
       - 4    STATEMENT ANALYSIS     ------------------     4
       - 5    FORECASTING            ------------------     5
       - 6    CAPITAL BUDGETING      ------------------     6
       - 7    FINANCING              ------------------     7
       - 8    WORKING CAPITAL        ------------------     8
       - 9    QUIT                   ------------------     9
     ----------------------------------------------------------
         Select a Category by Number and press <RET>
================================================================
```

5. Select one of the main categories shown above by **typing one** of the numbers from 1 - 9 and pressing <RET>.

6. You will now see a sub-menu containing the models for the category you selected in 5 above.

7. Select by number the model you wish to run and press <RET>.

8. The model will appear on the screen with a menu similar to the menus in Lotus.

9. At this point you should consult the chapter pertaining to the model that you have on the screen in order to fully understand the menu options and how to use the model.

Remember the above nine steps have been presented for persons knowledgeable about computers and spreadsheets. Even if you are experienced, it is recommended that you read Chapter 3 prior to using the CMF software. For those inexperienced, Chapters 2 and 3 will be required.

CROSS-REFERENCE TO SELECTED FINANCIAL TEXTS

For convenience, the CMF models are cross-referenced to selected financial texts. Exhibit I-4 immediately below lists several popular financial texts and a key code used to cross-reference them. Exhibit I-5, uses the key and cross-references the CMF models to corresponding chapters in these texts.

EXHIBIT I-4

KEY	TEXT
G	<u>Basic Managerial Finance</u> by Lawrence J. Gitman, Third Ed., Harper and Row, 1992.
B&H	<u>Foundations of Financial Management</u> by Stanley Block and Geoffrey Hirt, Sixth Ed., Irwin Publishers, 1992
RW&J	<u>Fundamentals of Corporate Finance</u> by Stephen Ross, Randolph Westerfield and Bradford Jordan, Second Edition, Richard D. Irwin, 1993.
B	<u>Fundamentals of Financial Management</u> by Eugene F. Brigham, Sixth Ed., 1992
B&G	<u>Financial Management: Theory and Practice</u> by Eugene Brigham and Louis C. Gapenski, Sixth Ed., The Dryden Press, 1991.

Each model is cross-referenced to a chapter or chapters in the above texts. The referenced chapter provides coverage of the financial theory and concepts relevant to the model. For example, financial material pertaining to time value of money (TIMEVAL) is found in chapter 9 of the Block and Hirt text.

While users will be able to <u>mechanically</u> operate the CMF software by using this manual, a proper application of the model and a correct interpretation of the results can only be assured if the user has a thorough understanding of the underlying financial concepts. Without such financial understanding, the models may easily be misapplied or the results misinterpreted.

All users should have a proper financial understanding of a subject prior to using the CMF model pertaining to that subject.

EXHIBIT I-5

CHAPTERS IN SELECTED FINANCIAL TEXTS

MODEL/TEXT	B&H	RW&J	G	B&G	B
TIMEVAL	9	5	11	6	5
ANNUITY	9	5	11	6	5
PERPETUY	9	5	11	6	5
TABLE	9	5	11	6	5
COMPFREQ	9	5	11	6	5
BETA	11	11	12	5	4
PORT	11	11	12	5	4
BOND	10	6	12	7	6
MORT	10	6	12	7	6
LEASE	10	6	12	7	6
PREFER	10	6	12	7	6
STOCK	10	6	12	7	6
FINSTATE	2	2	4	2	2
RATIO	3	3	4	22	2
COMSIZE	3	3	4	22	2
FUNDSFLO	3	3	4	22	16
PLAN	4	4	6	23	16
CASHBUD	4	17	6	23	9
GROWTH	N/A	4	N/A	23	N/A
CAPBUD	12	7,8,9	14,15	9,10	8
LEASEBUY	16	23	19	17	15
COSTCAP	11	14	13	8	7
LEVERAGE	5	9	5	13	11
EOQ	7	19	9	21	19
CASHBAL	7	17	N/A	20	18

KEY	AUTHORS
B&H	Block and Hirt
RW&J	Ross, Westerfield and Jordan
G	Gitman
B&G	Brigham & Gapenski
B	Brigham

SUMMARY

This chapter deals primarily with computer fundamentals such as the handling of floppy diskettes, installing the CMF software and backing-up the CMF software.

Because most recent computers have Hard Disks, **the discussion in this chapter assumes that the user has a computer with a hard disk.** If such assumption is not correct, consult your DOS manual or computer lab assistant for help on backing up your CMF software from one floppy diskette to another. If you do not have a hard disk computer, you should utilize your back-up copy when running CMF.

HANDLING FLOPPY DISKETTES

Floppy diskettes (or "disks" or "floppies" as they are often called) are generally 3.5 inches in diameter (older computer models had 5.25 inch disk drives and some still provide this size in addition to the 3.5 inch size). Diskettes provide storage for data or programs. A computer, once turned off, "forgets" any data that you have input. Therefore a means of preserving data that is not dependent upon electricity and leaving your computer turned on forever is necessary. Floppies provide an economic and reasonably convenient means of providing this preservation service.

Floppy diskettes appear fragile and, in this case, appearances are not deceiving. They must be handled with care. Generally common sense will provide you with enough of a guideline as to how to treat floppy diskettes. To supplement common sense, the following "do nots" are offered:

Do not spill coffee or other liquids on diskettes.

Do not unnecessarily expose them to dust or dirt.

Do not allow them to come into close proximity with magnets.

Do not place them in hot areas. Keep them away from heat such as radiators, closed cars in the summer, etc.

Do not bend them.

In addition to the "do nots", a universal "DO"

DO BACK-UP ANY FILES OR DATA THAT ARE IMPORTANT TO YOU

A subsequent section details how to "back-up" the CMF templates.

Chapter 2 COMPUTER BASICS

INSTALLING THE CMF SOFTWARE
To run the CMF software from your hard disk, you must first install the software. Do the following to install CMF to a hard disk:

1. Boot up your computer. At the **C>** prompt (generally the drive designation for a hard disk -- if yours is different make sure that you are at the proper prompt) type the following: **CD \<RET>**. (This will ensure that you are in the "root" directory.)

2. At the **C>** prompt type **MKDIR CMF<RET>**. (This command makes a subdirectory on drive C named CMF.)

3. At the **C>** prompt, type **CD CMF<RET>**. This command changes the directory from the root directory to the subdirectory named CMF.

4. At the **C:\CMF** prompt type: **A:<RET>**. (This command returns you to Drive A.) You should now be at the A> prompt.

5. Insert the CMF diskette into Drive A and close the disk drive door. At the A> prompt type: **COPY *.* C:<RET>**. (This command will copy all of the files from the CMF diskette in Drive A to Drive C.) Specifically, all files will be copied to the CMF subdirectory on drive C.

6. All files have now been copied to the hard disk in the subdirectory CMF. You now should back-up your CMF software.

BACKING-UP YOUR CMF SOFTWARE
Before using your CMF software, a back-up copy of the CMF software should be made. In order to make a back-up copy you will require one blank diskette.

>**Make sure that the diskette does not contain any data. Further, make sure that it is a formatted diskette.**

If the diskette is not formatted, it cannot accept information. If you do not know how to format a diskette, consult your computer lab assistant or your MS DOS manual.

>**BE CAREFUL: Formatting a diskette destroys all information on that diskette. Improper use of the formatting command can erase information on your hard drive.**

To back-up your CMF software, follow the following steps:

1. Place the formatted but empty diskette into Drive A.

2. Change to the C: drive if you are not already there by typing **C:<RET>**.

3. Change to the C:\CMF subdirectory (if you are already not there by typing: **CD\CMF<RET>**

4. At the prompt C:\CMF type **copy *.* A:<RET>**.

5. After all the files have been copied from the CMF directory to the diskette in Drive A, remove the diskette from Drive A, label it as your working copy of CMF and place your original copy of CMF safely away in storage.

6. You are now ready to load Lotus 1-2-3 and run CMF. Refer to the next chapter for detailed instructions on running CMF.

Chapter 3 HOW TO USE CMF

SUMMARY

The purpose of this chapter is to provide a comprehensive overview as to how to use the Computer Models in Finance (CMF) templates. This chapter should be **read before using CMF** and used as a reference source when questions or problems arise.

HOW TO LOAD CMF

The following instructions assume a hard-disk system with CMF installed in the CMF subdirectory as outlined in the previous chapter.

For users unfamiliar with the CMF software, the CMF MAIN MENU should be accessed first.

> **When reference is made to the CMF diskette below, it means either the CMF subdirectory on the Hard Disk or the CMF back-up disk.**

All the templates to be presented in this book are available from the MAIN MENU. To get to the MAIN MENU, do the following:

1. LOAD LOTUS 1-2-3
   It is assumed that you know how to load 1-2-3. If not, consult your computer lab assistant for directions as to how to load Lotus 1-2-3.

2. CHANGE THE DIRECTORY
   You must tell Lotus where to find the CMF software. To do so, type: **/FD\CMF<RET>**. The "/" brings up the Lotus menu. The "**FD**" is the file directory menu choice to make when you wish to change directories. You are changing to the CMF directory (or sub-directory).

3. LOAD THE CMF SOFTWARE
   At the Lotus 1-2-3 spreadsheet prompt type **/FR** (this is the Lotus File Retrieve command). The Lotus 1-2-3 software will prompt you for a filename. Type **FINANCE<RET>**.

At this point, CMF should have loaded and you should see the title screen as shown on the next page as Exhibit III-1.

EXHIBIT III-1

```
================================================================
$\                    COMPUTER MODELS IN FINANCE              /$
$$$\                 ===============================         /$$$
$$$$$\                  A Series of Templates               /$$$$$
$$$$$$$\                   Designed to Solve               /$$$$$$$
$$$$$$$$$\           Financial Management Problems        /$$$$$$$$$
$$$$$$$$$$$                                               $$$$$$$$$$$
$$$$$$$$$/                     developed by              \$$$$$$$$$
$$$$$$$/                  Lawrence E. McLean, PhD         \$$$$$$$
$$$$$/                                                      \$$$$$
$$$/                    Fayetteville State University         \$$$
$/                          Fayetteville, NC                    \$
================================================================
================================================================
          Copyright (C) by Macmillan Publishing Company, 1994

                             CMF 2.00
================================================================
                   Press <RET> to go to MAIN MENU
================================================================
```

If you cannot load the CMF software, it is probably because Lotus cannot find the file FINANCE. Repeat steps 2 and 3 above.

ACCESSING CMF TEMPLATES

There are two ways of accessing the CMF templates: 1) using the CMF menu system or 2) using the Lotus 1-2-3 "File Retrieve" command. Most users will use the menu system. If you use the templates on a regular basis and you know the file names, then you might be more comfortable accessing files directly.

1. ACCESSING TEMPLATES VIA THE MENU SYSTEM
   When you have loaded CMF via either of the procedures outlined above, a software title frame will appear on the screen. A representation of this frame is shown above as EXHIBIT III-1.

Pressing the <RET> key will move you to the MAIN MENU frame which appears as EXHIBIT III-2.

EXHIBIT III-2

```
================================================================
                          MAIN MENU
================================================================
   Number      Category                                  Number
   -------------------------------------------------------------
      - 1    TIME VALUE OF MONEY   ------------------      1
      - 2    RISK AND RETURN       ------------------      2
      - 3    VALUATION             ------------------      3
      - 4    STATEMENT ANALYSIS    ------------------      4
      - 5    FORECASTING           ------------------      5
      - 6    CAPITAL BUDGETING     ------------------      6
      - 7    FINANCING             ------------------      7
      - 8    WORKING CAPITAL       ------------------      8
      - 9    QUIT                  ------------------      9
   -------------------------------------------------------------
        Select a Category by Number and press <RET>
================================================================
```

The selections 1 - 8 from the MAIN MENU above will bring SUB-MENUS to the screen. Selection number 9 will erase the screen and return the user to a blank Lotus 1-2-3 worksheet.

From the MAIN MENU frame, you choose the number of the class of templates you wish to use. For example, from EXHIBIT III-2 above, if you were interested in TIME VALUE OF MONEY, you would type **1<RET>**. This choice would bring the TIME VALUE OF MONEY SUB-MENU to the screen.

A SUB-MENU is a collection of functionally-related templates. Each SUB-MENU offers at least two software templates. As an example, the TIME VALUE OF MONEY SUB-MENU appears on the screen as shown in Exhibit III-3.

EXHIBIT III-3

```
================================================================
                    TIME VALUE OF MONEY
================================================================
           Category                       Name        Number
----------------------------------------------------------------
     -     Present and Future Value      TIMEVAL         1
     -     Annuities                     ANNUITY         2
     -     Perpetuities                  PERPETUY        3
     -     Time Value Tables             TABLE           4
     -     Compounding Frequency         COMPFREQ        5
     -
     -
     -     RETURN TO MAIN MENU                           8
     -     QUIT                                          9
----------------------------------------------------------------
           Select a Category by Number and press <RET>
================================================================
```

Choosing numbers 1 - 5 from the TIME VALUE OF MONEY SUB-MENU above brings the corresponding financial template to the screen. Choosing 8 returns the user to the MAIN MENU, while 9 returns the user to a blank Lotus 1-2-3 spreadsheet.

Use of the menu system is recommended for most. It enables users to easily move amongst the financial templates without having to memorize the template names.

2. <u>ACCESSING TEMPLATES DIRECTLY WITH THE 1-2-3 "FILE RETRIEVE" COMMAND</u>   Once you become familiar with the CMF software you may wish to bypass the MAIN MENU (shown as EXHIBIT III-2) when loading templates or moving between templates. In order to access models directly, it is necessary to know the following:

   1. The names of the models

   2. The CMF diskette on which the model resides

This information is available in several locations. Probably the most convenient location is Exhibit I-1 in Chapter 1.

Chapter 3: How to Use CMF   19

The manner in which you access templates directly depends upon where you are in the Lotus-CMF process:

<u>If you have loaded Lotus but have not entered the CMF software:</u> You may load any of the CMF templates by typing from the command line of Lotus the following: **/FR**, which is the File Retrieve command in Lotus. Lotus will then show (in Lotus menu format) the files on disk. You may move the cursor to the file you wish to load and press <RET>. Or you may type the name of the file (e.g., BOND) followed by <RET>. Either method will load the file. **Remember, in order for you to find the CMF files, you must have changed the default directory in Lotus to the CMF directory (see above under HOW TO LOAD CMF.**

<u>If you have loaded CMF and wish to move from one CMF template to another:</u> You may either get to the next template by going back to the MAIN MENU, or you may go directly to the template as described in the above paragraph. For directions on how to do this, see LEAVING THE TEMPLATE on page 26.

CMF TEMPLATE MENU INFORMATION

<u>EXPLANATION OF A TEMPLATE MENU</u>
All CMF templates are menu-driven. When a template is loaded, a TEMPLATE MENU appears at the top of the Lotus screen. Whenever a TEMPLATE MENU appears, the program waits for the user to make a selection. An example of a TEMPLATE MENU is shown as EXHIBIT III-4.

<u>EXHIBIT III-4</u>

TEMPLATE MENU

(FACSIMILE OF THE COMPUTER MONITOR)

                                                    CMD MENU
   OLD DATA   NEW DATA   VIEW   GRAPH   PRINT   HELP   END
   Modify existing data

If you have used Lotus before, you should be familiar with the operation of these menus. The boldfaced type of OLD DATA indicates that the cursor resides on this choice. On the line immediately below the TEMPLATE MENU line is a short explanation of the OLD DATA command. In the example above, the choice of OLD DATA allows you to "modify existing data." You may select the command under the cursor by typing <RET> (pressing the RETURN key). You may move the cursor to a different command by using the CURSOR MOVEMENT KEYS (the arrow keys on the numeric key pad on the right of the keyboard). As you move the cursor, the line below (which shows the explanation of the command the cursor is on) changes.

An alternative method for selecting a command from a TEMPLATE MENU is to type the first letter of the command. For example, if you want the GRAPH option, type "G" or "g." Even though the cursor resides on OLD DATA, GRAPH will be selected.

The upper-right-hand portion of the screen shows CMD MENU (command menu). This indicator means that you are in a menu specifically designed for the financial template. These menus look and operate much like the standard Lotus menus with one exception:

IMPORTANT: **DO NOT USE THE <ESC> KEY IN TEMPLATE MENUS !!**

Regular users of Lotus may be accustomed to employing the <ESC> key to move back to the previous menu level. While this technique works with Lotus menus, it will not work with TEMPLATE MENUS. Using the <ESC> key with a TEMPLATE MENU will cause an ERROR condition and remove you from the program. **The <ESC> key should not be used while in CMF templates.** (One small exception is discussed under ESCAPE KEY in the section below on special CMF keys (page 29.)

SAVING DATA
No template except the Financial Statements (FINSTATE) template provides you with a SAVE menu choice. This template is an exception because it deals with large amounts of information and provides the input means for the four other templates in the Statement Analysis section.

USERS SHOULD NOT ATTEMPT TO SAVE DATA WHERE THIS OPTION IS NOT PROVIDED IN A TEMPLATE MENU.

When you use a template which does not have a SAVE option, input the data and print it out. If you need to work with it again, you must re-input the data. Generally the templates with no SAVE option deal with relatively small amounts of input.

SAVING TEMPLATES
No provision is made for saving templates. It is unnecessary.

USERS SHOULD NEVER TRY TO SAVE ANYTHING TO AN EXISTING TEMPLATE

Saving anything to a template file will overwrite the template and destroy or modify its contents. If a template file is ever overwritten, go to your original CMF disk and copy the original version of the template to your damaged working copy. Do this immediately. Do not try to utilize the damaged version.

VIEWING DATA
Larger templates have VIEW options in the TEMPLATE MENU. This option enables the user to see parts of the solution that cannot be seen on the initial screen. CURSOR MOVEMENT KEYS (see page 30) enable movement within the VIEW area. To return to the template menu, press <RET>.

PRINTING DATA
Many of the templates have PRINT options in the TEMPLATE MENU. You may, however, print output from all templates.

> <u>If the TEMPLATE MENU contains a PRINT option:</u> To print output, merely choose that option from the TEMPLATE MENU.
>
> <u>If there is no PRINT option:</u> Those templates that do not include a PRINT option involve small amounts of potential output data. Printed output can be obtained by typing **<SHIFT>PRTSC**. That is, while holding down the SHIFT (or CAPS) key, depress the PrtSc or PrintScreen key (usually located near the right-hand SHIFT key). This action will print what is visible on your computer monitor (including the border area of the Lotus 1-2-3 spreadsheet).

The **<SHIFT>PRTSC** key may be used even when a template has a PRINT option. Sometimes only a small amount of data is required in printed form. When this is the case, using this key is more efficient than printing the entire results. Two templates where you may wish to print less than the entire output are the TIMEVAL and RATIO templates. The TIMEVAL PRINT option prints all time periods from 0 - 50. The RATIO PRINT option prints the income statement, the balance sheet and the ratios. Using the **<SHIFT>PRTSC** key allows you to target those results that you wish to obtain in "hard copy." There may be instances in other templates where the **<SHIFT>PRTSC** key may be used to your advantage.

CAUTION: If there is any chance you may want to print something, TURN YOUR PRINTER ON when you turn your computer on.

GRAPHING DATA

Many of the TEMPLATE MENUS have GRAPH options. Not all computer configurations, however, are capable of seeing Lotus graphs. If you cannot get graphed data on the screen, you either have to switch computers, spend more money to remedy the problem or forget about the GRAPH option included in the CMF templates.

When you select GRAPH you will see a graph (if only one graph exists for that template) or a sub-menu of graph names (where multiple graphs exist). To select one of multiple graphs, move the cursor over your choice and press <RET>. IMPORTANT: you must select the graph in this manner. **You cannot type the first letter of the name and retrieve the graph.** After you are finished viewing a graph, press <RET>, and you will be returned to the TEMPLATE MENU.

It should be noted that the documentation on templates contained in subsequent chapters does not provide an explanation of the graphs included. If you have the capability of viewing graphs, explore each template's graphs. Sometimes graphs show relationships in data or between variables that are missed from a review of the numbers.

There is no provision included in any of the CMF templates for printing graphs to a printer. The best you can do is view graphs on the screen. Graphs are set up to work with monochrome monitors. Thus, **even if you are using a color monitor you will see the graph in black and white.**

LEAVING THE TEMPLATE

All templates have an END menu option which allows several choices for leaving the template. The sub-menu that appears after selection of the END option includes the following choices:

    RETURN - Do Not Leave This Template -- Return to Processing
    MAIN MENU - Go to MAIN MENU of Financial Software
    NEW FILE - Go Directly to Another Finance Template
    QUIT - Go to Lotus spreadsheet (LEAVE FINANCE)

RETURN is a "change-of-mind" option. MAIN MENU AND NEW FILE are both routes to another CMF template. The NEW FILE option allows the user to choose another CMF file and go directly to it (bypassing the MAIN MENU route). QUIT leaves the CMF program entirely and returns the user to a blank spreadsheet for continued processing in Lotus.

RESTARTING THE PROGRAM

While it should not happen, it is possible that you may be removed from the automatic processing that drives the CMF template. This condition is not particularly serious, is easy to remedy, and involves no data loss.

<u>REMOVED FROM PROGRAM</u>
The "removed from program" condition is often a subtle one. It does not involve your screen going blank or even changing appearance very much. When it occurs, you may not even know that you are "removed from the program" until the computer fails to return a TEMPLATE MENU to the screen or respond in the manner you are expecting. By looking up at the top right-hand corner of the screen, you will be able to tell whether you have been removed from the program. You should always see one of the following three commands in the upper-right:

>   CMD MENU - Program is at a TEMPLATE MENU awaiting user selection.
>   CMD READY - Program is awaiting keyboard entry from user.
>   WAIT (blinking) - Indicates that program is calculating. This condition will (without any user actions) become CMD MENU when the calculation is done.

If any other message appears in the upper-right-hand corner, it means that you have been "removed from the program." (The most common messages are ERROR or the READY command.)

<u>WHAT TO DO IF REMOVED FROM THE PROGRAM</u>
If removed from the program, merely type **\<ALT\> B**. That is, while holding down the ALT key (lower-left portion of the keyboard), depress the letter B (or small b). This will cause the financial template to BEGIN again. You will be returned to the TEMPLATE MENU. Any data already input remains intact and usable. If typing **\<ALT\> B** causes the computer to "beep" at you, and the template cannot be restarted, type **\<ESC\>** and then type **\<ALT\> B**. Th   sequence should restart the template.

>   **CAUTION:** Do not type \<ALT\> B <u>**unless you have been removed for the program!**</u>

Unpredictable results may occur if the \<ALT\> B command is used while "not removed from the program." One result that may occur is a "locked" computer. A "locked" computer is a situation where the computer will not respond to any commands. To escape this condition, the user must re-start the computer, reload Lotus 1-2-3 and reload the CMF software. Any data that had been entered into the CMF model and not saved to diskette will have to be re-entered.

HOW TO INPUT DATA INTO CMF TEMPLATES

<u>PERCENTAGES</u> are entered as decimals or as numbers with the percentage sign pressed. For example, 11.25% can be entered as **.1125<RET>** or **11.25%<RET>**.

<u>DOLLARS</u> are entered without dollar signs or commas. Decimal points are allowed, but only one to a number.

<u>NUMBERS</u> (including Percentages and Dollars) may be preceded by + or - signs. Numbers may also be entered as formulas. For example 5-3 is the same as entering 2. The other mathematical operators are +, /, and *. The latter two represent division and multiplication, respectively. An entry is completed by pressing **<RET>** or one of the **CURSOR MOVEMENT KEYS.**

Formulas may also be used to enter data. For example, +C3+2 is equivalent to adding the contents of cell C3 and the number 2. The result will appear in the cell occupied by the cursor. (For more information on Lotus formulas, consult the Lotus manual.)

SPECIAL KEYS THAT ARE USED IN CMF

RETURN is the Return or Enter key on your computer keyboard. The key is located in the right-center portion of the keyboard. Throughout the text, this key will be referred to as <RET>. This key serves both as a **DATA ENTRY KEY** and as the **CALCULATE KEY** (see below).

CURSOR MOVEMENT KEYS are located on the numerical key pad (grouping of keys on the right-hand side of the keyboard). The keys 2,4,8 and 6 all move the cursor one cell in the direction indicated by the arrow. These keys also are **DATA ENTRY KEYS**.

DATA ENTRY KEYS are keys which enter data. Either the **RETURN** key or the **CURSOR MOVEMENT KEYS** can enter data. Move the cursor to an input cell, type data and enter the data either by typing **<RET>** or by using the **CURSOR MOVEMENT KEYS** to move the cursor to the next input cell.

CALCULATE KEY is the **<RET> key.** In order to update the results, you must recalculate the template. When in data input mode, merely type <RET> without entering any data. The "WAIT" signal will flash in the upper-right-hand corner of the Lotus spreadsheet until the calculation is completed.

PRINT KEY is the **<SHIFT>PRTSC** key. While holding down the SHIFT (CAPS) key, depress the "PrtSc" or "PrintScreen" key (usually located near the right-hand SHIFT key). This key will cause whatever is shown on the monitor to be printed. This key is available in all templates and may be used at any point in the template. Your printer, of course, should be turned on prior to using this key.

RESTART KEY may be required should you somehow be removed from the program. This key is **<ALT> B** and is executed by holding down the "Alt" on the lower-left portion of your keyboard while depressing the letter "B" or "b." This action will restart the template's program and return you to the TEMPLATE MENU commands. After a restart, choose the relevant option to return to the point you stopped entering data. Previously entered data will be intact and will not have to be re-entered.

ESCAPE KEY is labeled as "Esc" on the upper-left portion of your keyboard. This key, referred to in the text as <ESC>, will only be needed if you are unable to restart your template per the instructions above. If this is the case, press <ESC> followed by <ALT> B and the template will restart. **This is the only time when the ESCAPE key should be used in CMF.**

TEMPLATE APPLICATIONS

Subsequent chapters in this text consist of documentation and discussion of the individual templates. Space considerations limited the number and range of applications that could be demonstrated. Two comments regarding the flexibility of the templates and their usefulness in sensitivity analysis are in order:

FLEXIBILITY
At the end of each chapter a sample problem and solution is presented. The sample problem represents an attempt to assist the user in understanding how to utilize a particular template. Do not assume that the template can only solve the type of problem demonstrated. **The templates are capable of solving a wide range of problems.** The user is encouraged to apply the templates to other types of problems in addition to the ones demonstrated in this text.

SENSITIVITY ANALYSIS
An important part of "real-world" financial decision-making involves the use of sensitivity analysis. Sensitivity analysis explores the relative importance of variables and is an important tool used to assess risk. In effect, the decision-maker determines how "sensitive" a solution is to changes in the inputs to a problem. The CMF templates allow users to perform sensitivity analysis with relative ease. In some chapters sensitivity analysis is used in the solution to the sample problem. In virtually all templates and for all types of problems, sensitivity analysis may be performed by the user. **The user is encouraged to utilize sensitivity analysis even where the problem does not specifically request it.** Its use will produce a better understanding of the use and power of the templates, the technique of sensitivity analysis itself, and the relative importance of various inputs on the decision or outcome. This latter point is critical to effective financial management in the business world.

FOR ADDITIONAL INFORMATION CONSULT
YOUR LOTUS 1-2-3 MANUAL
OR
SUBSEQUENT CHAPTERS IN THIS TEXT

PART II:
TIME VALUE OF MONEY

CHAPTER	TOPIC	NAME	PAGE
4	Present and Future Value	TIMEVAL	33
5	Annuities	ANNUITY	37
6	Perpetuities	PERPETUY	39
7	Time Value Tables	TABLE	43
8	Compounding Frequency	COMPFREQ	45

Part II of the book presents five templates dealing with the time value of money.

The first three templates allow for the solution of present value, future value and internal rates of return problems for level (annuities) and unlevel cash flows and perpetuities (both conventional and constant growth rates to infinity).

The latter two allow the user to develop time value of money tables (present and future value) and to compare the impact of frequency of compounding on future value factors.

Chapter 4 PRESENT AND FUTURE VALUE

PURPOSE: To calculate the Present Value, Future Value or Internal Rate of Return (IRR) of single or multiple cash flows. The cash flows may be uneven.

LOADING THE TEMPLATE:
From the TIME VALUE OF MONEY sub-menu choose number: 1
From LOTUS choose file name: TIMEVAL

TEMPLATE MENU: Menu choices available and their functions are as follows:
    OLD DATA - input data via overtyping existing data
    NEW DATA - erase existing data and input new data
    VIEW - move around the spreadsheet to view output
    GRAPH - output shown in graph form
    PRINT - prints results for periods 0 - 50
    HELP - presents a help screen
    END - allows the user to leave this template

HOW TO INPUT DATA: Choose OLD DATA or NEW DATA menu option. Cursor will move to the first input field. (Note that input fields are generally shown on the screen between ">" and "<" symbols.) Input for this template is in the range of cells C4 - C61, excluding cells C6 - C10.

EXPLANATION OF CERTAIN INPUTS
    i - Interest rate to be used in calculations (Enter in decimal form)
    t - period cash flows will be converted to. Choose t=0 for **PRESENT VALUE** calculations; choose t greater than 0 for **FUTURE VALUE** calculations as of time period "t." See below for **INTERNAL RATE OF RETURN**.

CALCULATING THE RESULTS
While inputting data, press <RET> without entering any data. Calculation will be performed automatically by the program. The program will return to the TEMPLATE MENU after calculation is complete. IMPORTANT: Do not use the LOTUS <F9> key to calculate.

A NOTE ON PRINTING
The template menu has a print option that will print 51 time periods of data. For short problems, you may wish to use **<SHIFT> PRTSC** instead of the menu print option. See Chapter 3, "PRINTING DATA," for additional information.

INTERNAL RATE OF RETURN (IRR): The template will attempt to calculate an IRR whenever the Cash Flow in time period 0 is negative. This calculation will be made in addition to the PV or FV calculation requested. An error ("ERR") will result if LOTUS is unable to converge on a correct solution. In case of an error, there may be a way of forcing convergence (see A Supplementary Comment on IRR Calculations at the end of this chapter). Users may also try to "manually" calculate an IRR even when the period 0 cash flow is not negative (of course some cash flows must be negative). To determine the IRR "manually," set t = 0 and change interest rates until a PV = 0 (or very close to zero) is calculated. The interest rate (if any) that accomplishes this condition is the IRR.

TECHNICAL INFORMATION AND TEMPLATE LIMITATIONS
The template can only handle 51 time periods (periods 0 - 50). All cash flows are assumed to occur at the end of the time periods. The time-value FACTOR (TVF) is calculated as follows:

$$TVF = (1+i)^n$$

where i = interest rate and n = difference between "t" and the period in which the cash flow occurs.
VALUE equals the Cash Flow multiplied times the FACTOR.

PROBLEMS
Solve the following:

   a. future value of $200 after 10 years at 10% per year compounded annually.
   b. present value of $550 received after 4 years at 8%.
   c. present value at 12% of the following stream of cash flows: year 1, $100; year 2, $200; year 3, $300; year 4, $200; year 5, $100.
   d. future value of the cash flows in part e after 10 years.
   e. the internal rate of return (IRR) of the cash flows in part e if time period 0 has an outflow of $600.

SOLUTIONS:

PART a.
Choose the NEW DATA option. Enter .10 for i, 10 for t and $200 as the Cash Flow in period 0. To calculate, press <RET> without entering any numbers. The answer (shown in the upper-right-hand corner of the screen) is $518.75.

PART b.
Choose the NEW DATA option. Enter .08 for i; 0 for t and $550 for period 4. Press <RET> without entering any numbers to calculate. The answer (PV) is 404.27.

Chapter 4: Present and Future Value

PART c.
Choose the NEW DATA option. Enter .12 for i; 0 for t and the cash flows in the corresponding periods. The answer ($646.10) and the screen after calculation is shown on the following page as EXHIBIT IV-1.

EXHIBIT IV-1

SOLUTION TO PART c

```
=================================================================
<ALT B> to RESTART PROGRAM                    ****   SOLUTIONS:   ***
  i = >     12.00%   <  Interest Rate         * PV           $646.10
  t = >          0   <  0=PV; GREATER THAN 0=FV *IRR              NA
                                              * FV               NA
                                              ***********************
                                                         CUMULATIVE
PERIOD Cash Flow       FACTOR            VALUE             VALUE
-----------------------------------------------------------------
    0 >              <  1.000            $0.00             $0.00
    1 >     100      <  0.893            89.29             89.29
    2 >     200      <  0.797           159.44            248.72
    3 >     300      <  0.712           213.53            462.26
    4 >     200      <  0.636           127.10            589.36
    5 >     100      <  0.567            56.74            646.10
    6 >              <  0.507             0.00            646.10
                       -----------------------------------
```

PART d.
Choose OLD DATA (to preserve the input already in the template), enter 10 for t (by overtyping the zero) and calculate to get an FV of $2006.70

PART e.
Choose OLD DATA. Enter 0 for t and -600 for time period 0 (cell C11). Calculate. Note that an ERR now shows as the IRR solution. This ERR indicates that Lotus was unable to converge on a correct IRR solution. Because the IRR calculation uses the i value as its "guess" in an attempt to converge on a solution, if we can change the i value closer to the true IRR, LOTUS may be able to converge. Because the PV is positive at 12%, it means that the IRR must be a higher rate. Choose the OLD DATA option again. Enter .14 for i. Now the IRR algorithm converges, and the answer is 14.97%.

A SUPPLEMENTARY COMMENT ON IRR CALCULATIONS

The TIMEVAL template will attempt to solve for an IRR only when the time period 0 cash flow is negative. You may, however, solve IRR problems using the PV option of this template even when time period 0 cash flow is not negative. By definition, the IRR is any interest rate that results in PV = 0. Knowing this information, the method discussed below will allow you to solve for any IRR.

You can solve for the Internal Rate of Return by changing the interest rate, i, and recalculating until an i is found that results in PV = 0. This method is identical to, although easier than, the guessing used to solve IRR problems with a present value table or a hand-held calculator. If you try this approach, you will find that PV is close, but not equal, to zero at an interest rate of 14.97% (PV = -$0.05). This finding does not represent a discrepancy between Lotus' IRR function and your "guessing" approach. It is due to the rounding used in the answers in the TIMEVAL template. The answer has been rounded off from eight or more decimal places calculated by Lotus. You could, by "guessing," find that interest rate that would cause PV to equal zero (or at least get within pennies of zero) by using interest rates beyond four decimal points. For example, guesses such as .14965 or .14967345 might be necessary. Although both of these numbers show up as i = 14.97% in the template, the unrounded entries are used in the calculations. You might try one of these numbers to view a small change in the PV.

Remember that the IRR calculation will only be attempted by the template when the time period 0 cash flow is negative. If you wish to solve for an IRR when this condition is not met, you must use the "guessing" approach described above.

Chapter 5 ANNUITIES

PURPOSE
To calculate the Present Value, Future Value, IRR (Effective Interest) or Payment of a stream of uniform cash flows (annuity). A "balloon" payment is possible in the final period.

LOADING THE TEMPLATE
From the TIME VALUE OF MONEY sub-menu choose number: 2
From LOTUS choose file name: ANNUITY

TEMPLATE MENU
Menu choices available and their functions are as follows:
   DATA - input data via overtyping existing data
   HELP - presents a help screen
   END - allows the user to leave this template

HOW TO INPUT DATA
Choose DATA menu option. Cursor will move to the first input field. (Note that input fields are generally shown on the screen between ">" and "<" symbols.) Input for this template is in the range of cells C8 - C13.

EXPLANATION OF CERTAIN INPUTS
   UNKNOWN - Enter variable to solve for: PV=1; FV=2; r=3; PMT=4
   r - Interest rate in decimal form
   pv - Present Value of stream of cash flows
   fv - Payment in year n <u>in addition to</u> any pmt in the problem
   pmt - Uniform payments for "n" time periods
   n - Number of uniform payments

FUTURE VALUE PAYMENT AS "BALLOON" PAYMENT
When solving for any of the unknowns, the value of fv (Cell C11) is treated as an additional cash flow in period n. Thus it may be used, for example, as a "balloon" payment. Please note, however, that if you have a 10-period problem with 9 payments of 100 and a balloon of 1000 in the 10th year, you must enter pmt = 100; n = 10; and fv = 900 (because it is added to the 100 payment already made in year 10). Incorrect input of the balloon (fv) is a common problem in using this template.

CALCULATING THE RESULTS
While inputting data, press <RET> without entering any data. Calculation will be performed automatically by the program. The program will return to the TEMPLATE MENU after calculation is complete. IMPORTANT: Do not use the LOTUS <F9> key to calculate.

TECHNICAL INFORMATION AND TEMPLATE LIMITATIONS
All cash flows are assumed to take place at the end of a time period. An fv entry is assumed in period n (and is added to any pmt that may occur in that time period).

PROBLEMS
Solve the following:
- a. future value of $100 a year for 30 years at 10% per year compounded annually.
- b. present value of $100 a year for 30 years at 10%.
- c. payments necessary to accumulate $100,000 30 years from now if the savings earn 10% interest compounded annually.

SOLUTIONS

PART a.
Choose the DATA menu option and input the following data: 2 for UNKNOWN, .10 for r, 100 for pmt and 30 for n. Calculate by typing <RET> without entering any data, and the answer of $16,449.40 will appear in the upper-right-hand corner of the screen. The screen will appear as follows:

```
===============================================================
                        ************    SOLUTION    *************
                           FUTURE VALUE            $16,449.40
                           EFFECTIVE INT                   NA
            INPUT:      ******************************************
---------------------------------------------------------------
UNKNOWN  |         2     Unknown Variable (1=PV, 2=FV, 3=r, 4=PMT)
r        |    10.00%     Interest Rate
pv       |               Present Value
fv       |               Future Value or "Balloon" payment
pmt      |   $100.00     Payment or Receipt per period
n        |        30     Number of level cash flows
---------------------------------------------------------------
```

PART b.
Choose the DATA option. Move the cursor to UNKNOWN and overtype the 2 with 1. Calculate. The answer will be $942.69.

PART c.
Choose the DATA option. Overtype the UNKNOWN with 4 and n with 30. Enter fv as 100,000. Calculate. The answer will be $(607.92). The negative number means that you must save (deposit) this amount.

Chapter 6 PERPETUITIES

PURPOSE: To calculate market value, interest rate, payment or growth rate of a perpetuity or constant growth-rate stream to infinity. (This model is very similar to the Preferred Stock model, PREFER, in Chapter 14.)

LOADING THE TEMPLATE
From the TIME VALUE OF MONEY sub-menu choose number: 3
From LOTUS choose file name: PERPETUY

TEMPLATE MENU: Menu choices available are as follows:
   DATA - input data
   HELP - presents a help screen
   END - allows the user to leave this template

HOW TO INPUT DATA: Choose DATA menu option. Cursor will move to the first input field. (Note that input fields are generally shown on the screen between ">" and "<" symbols.) Input for this template is in the range of cells C8 - C12.

EXPLANATION OF CERTAIN INPUTS
   Unknown - Enter number of unknown variable: PV = 1; g = 2; r = 3; PMT = 4.
   r - Interest rate or effective return
   PV - Current market value of the perpetuity
   g - Constant growth rate of the cash flow stream (0 for standard perpetuity)
   pmt - Amount of cash flow in first period

CALCULATING THE RESULTS
While inputting data, press <RET> without entering any data. Calculation will be performed automatically by the program. The program will return to the TEMPLATE MENU after calculation is complete. IMPORTANT: Do not use the LOTUS <F9> key to calculate.

TECHNICAL INFORMATION AND TEMPLATE LIMITATIONS
The formula for calculating the perpetuity is the Gordon Growth Model:

$$PV = pmt(1)/(r - g)$$

where pmt(1) is the cash flow in the first time period, and the other variables are defined as above. The standard perpetuity is a special case of this formula where g = 0.

If the growth rate, g, is greater than the interest rate, r, the problem is not solvable, and an error is returned as the solution.

PROBLEMS:

Problem 1:
What is the present value of a constant stream of $100 per year to infinity if the required return on similar risk securities is 10%?

Problem 2:
How much more would this stream be worth if it grew at a rate of 3% per year?

Problem 3:
If the market requires a 10% return, what constant payment to infinity would be required to make an asset worth $2,000?

SOLUTIONS:

Problem 1:
Choose the DATA option and input the following information: Unknown = 1, r = .10 and pmt = 100. After calculation, the computer screen appears as shown below. The answer, shown in the upper right-hand corner of the screen, is $1,000.00.

```
    <ALT> B to RESTART              PERPETUITY
==============================================================
                                ************  SOLUTION  ********
                                PRESENT VALUE =            $1,000.00
                                EFF. INTEREST =                  NA
                 INPUT:         *************************************
    --------------------------------------------------------------
    UNKNOWN   |           1    | Unknown Variable (1=PV,2=g,3=r,4=PMT)
    r         |      10.00%    | Interest Rate
    pv        |                | Present Value
    g         |                | Constant Growth Rate (percentage)
    pmt       |      $100.00   | First payment
    --------------------------------------------------------------
```

Chapter 6: Perpetuities

Problem 2:
Choose the DATA option and merely input .03 for g. The solution is $1,428.57, and the screen should appear as follows:

```
<ALT> B to RESTART              PERPETUITY
================================================================
                              ************   SOLUTION   ********
                              PRESENT VALUE =          $1,428.57
                              EFF. INTEREST =                 NA
                 INPUT:       ************************************
----------------------------------------------------------------
UNKNOWN     |          1     | Unknown Variable (1=PV,2=g,3=r,4=PMT)
  r         |     10.00%     | Interest Rate
  pv        |                | Present Value
  g         |      3.00%     | Constant Growth Rate (percentage)
  pmt       |    $100.00     | First payment
----------------------------------------------------------------
```

Problem 3:
Choose the DATA option and overtype UNKNOWN with 2 and put 2000 in for pv and 100 in for pmt. The solution is 5.00% and the screen should appear as follows:

```
<ALT> B to RESTART              PERPETUITY
================================================================
                              ************   SOLUTION   ********
                              PRESENT VALUE =                 NA
                              GROWTH                       5.00%
                 INPUT:       ************************************
----------------------------------------------------------------
UNKNOWN     |          2     | Unknown Variable (1=PV, 2=g, 3=r, 4=PMT)
  r         |     10.00%     | Interest Rate
  pv        |  $2,000.00     | Present Value
  g         |                | Constant Growth Rate (percentage)
  pmt       |    $100.00     | First payment
----------------------------------------------------------------
```

Chapter 7 TIME VALUE TABLES

PURPOSE
To create a table of time value of money factors. Present and Future Value of single sums and annuities of $1.00 are calculated.

LOADING THE TEMPLATE
From the TIME VALUE OF MONEY sub-menu choose number: 4
From LOTUS choose file name: TABLE

TEMPLATE MENU
Menu choices available and their functions are as follows:
   DATA - input data
   VIEW - move around the spreadsheet to view table values
   GRAPH - output shown in graph form
   PRINT - prints entire table
   END - allows the user to leave this template

HOW TO INPUT DATA
Choose DATA menu option. Cursor will move to the first input field. (Note that input fields are generally shown on the screen between ">" and "<" symbols.) Input for this template is in the range of cells C3-C4.

EXPLANATION OF CERTAIN INPUTS

   Interest - Interest rate entered in decimal form
   Beg. Per. - First period shown in the table. Almost always
       will be 1. If you need values for time periods further
       into the future than shown in the table, increase the
       entry in this field.

CALCULATING THE RESULTS
While inputting data, press <RET> without entering any data. Calculation will be performed automatically by the program. The program will return to the TEMPLATE MENU after calculation is complete. IMPORTANT: Do not use the LOTUS <F9> key to calculate.

TECHNICAL INFORMATION AND TEMPLATE LIMITATIONS
All cash flows are assumed to occur at the end of the time period. The table shows 30 single time periods and then 4 periods equally spaced 5 periods apart. For example, if the first time period is 1, then values will be calculated for periods 1-30, 35, 40, 45 and 50.

PROBLEM
For 10% interest, find the present and future value factors of a single sum of $1.00 received at the end of 10 years. Do the same for an annuity of $1.00 per year.

SOLUTION
Choose DATA option from menu. Enter .10 for Interest and 1 for Beg. Per. Calculate and look up the values from the 10-period row. The answers are as follows:

	PV	FV
SINGLE SUM:	0.3855	2.3579
ANNUITY:	6.1446	15.9374

Input and output from this template are below:

```
=================================================================
Interest    >       10.00% <  Enter Interest Rate
Beg. Per.   >            1 <  Enter First Time Period -- Usually 1
-----------------------------------------------------------------
    TIME VALUE TABLES        INTEREST RATE:         10.00%
=================================================================
              VALUE OF SINGLE SUM         VALUE OF AN ANNUITY
              -------------------         -------------------
TIME PERIOD   PRESENT      FUTURE         PRESENT      FUTURE
-----------------------------------------------------------------
     1        0.9091       1.1000         0.9091       1.0000
     2        0.8264       1.2100         1.7355       2.1000
     3        0.7513       1.3310         2.4869       3.3100
     4        0.6830       1.4641         3.1699       4.6410
     5        0.6209       1.6105         3.7908       6.1051
     6        0.5645       1.7716         4.3553       7.7156
     7        0.5132       1.9487         4.8684       9.4872
     8        0.4665       2.1436         5.3349      11.4359
     9        0.4241       2.3579         5.7590      13.5795
    10        0.3855       2.5937         6.1446      15.9374
            /////////////////////////////////////////////////////
                        Periods 11 - 24 not shown
            /////////////////////////////////////////////////////
    25        0.0923      10.8347         9.0770      98.3471
    26        0.0839      11.9182         9.1609     109.1818
    27        0.0763      13.1100         9.2372     121.0999
    28        0.0693      14.4210         9.3066     134.2099
    29        0.0630      15.8631         9.3696     148.6309
    30        0.0573      17.4494         9.4269     164.4940
    35        0.0356      28.1024         9.6442     271.0244
    40        0.0221      45.2593         9.7791     442.5926
    45        0.0137      72.8905         9.8628     718.9048
    50        0.0085     117.3909         9.9148    1163.9085
=================================================================
```

Chapter 8 COMPOUNDING FREQUENCY

PURPOSE: To compare the effects of different compounding frequencies on future value.

LOADING THE TEMPLATE
From the TIME VALUE OF MONEY sub-menu choose number: 5
From LOTUS choose file name: COMPFREQ

TEMPLATE MENU: Menu choices available are as follows:
   DATA - input data
   VIEW - move around the spreadsheet to view table values
   PRINT - prints entire table
   END - allows the user to leave this template

HOW TO INPUT DATA: Choose DATA menu option. Cursor will move to the first input field. (Note that input fields are generally shown on the screen between ">" and "<" symbols.) Input for this template is in the cells C3 and C4.

EXPLANATION OF CERTAIN INPUTS

   i - Enter interest rate.
   Per - First time period. This entry is usually 1, although
         higher numbers can be used to calculate periods further
         out.

CALCULATING THE RESULTS
While inputting data, press <RET> without entering any data. Calculation will be performed automatically by the program. The program will return to the TEMPLATE MENU after calculation is complete. IMPORTANT: Do not use the LOTUS <F9> key to calculate.

TECHNICAL INFORMATION AND TEMPLATE LIMITATIONS
The table will only calculate annual, quarterly, daily and continuous compounding. Although the table presents only the first 10 periods and then a series of 5-period intervals thereafter, this should not be a limitation because of the ability to modify Per, the beginning time period. (See Problem below for an example.)

PROBLEM:
If you can earn 12% interest compounded annually and 12% compounded daily, how much more will a dollar be worth in 10 years with the quarterly compounding? How much more in 50 years?
SOLUTION:
Choose the DATA option and input the following information:

        i = .12 and Per = 1.

After calculation, the computer screen appears as shown below as Exhibit VIII-1.

EXHIBIT VIII-1

```
 1      TIME VALUE FACTORS FOR COMPOUNDING MORE THAN ONCE PER YEAR
 2     ================================================================
 3      i = >            12.00% <  Enter Annual Interest Rate
 4      Per >                 1 <  Enter First Time Period -- Usually 1
 5     ----------------------------------------------------------------
 6             FUTURE VALUE FACTORS FOR A SINGLE SUM
 7     ================================================================
 8      ANNUAL INTEREST RATE =        12.00%
 9      PERIOD          ANNUAL       QUARTERLY        DAILY    CONTINUOUS
10     ----------------------------------------------------------------
11        1             1.120          1.126          1.127       1.127
12        2             1.254          1.267          1.271       1.271
13        3             1.405          1.426          1.433       1.433
14        4             1.574          1.605          1.616       1.616
15        5             1.762          1.806          1.822       1.822
16        6             1.974          2.033          2.054       2.054
17        7             2.211          2.288          2.316       2.316
18        8             2.476          2.575          2.611       2.612
19        9             2.773          2.898          2.944       2.945
20       10             3.106          3.262          3.319       3.320
       ----------------------------------------------------------------
```

A dollar compounded annually for 10 years at 12% interest will be worth $3.106 while compounded daily it will be worth $3.319.

To solve for 50 periods, merely choose the data option, input Per = 50 and calculate. The solution appears as Exhibit VIII-2 below.

EXHIBIT VIII-2

```
 1      TIME VALUE FACTORS FOR COMPOUNDING MORE THAN ONCE PER YEAR
 2     ================================================================
 3      i = >            12.00% <  Enter Annual Interest Rate
 4      Per >                50 <  Enter First Time Period--Usually 1
 5     ----------------------------------------------------------------
 6             FUTURE VALUE FACTORS FOR A SINGLE SUM
 7     ================================================================
 8      ANNUAL INTEREST RATE =        12.00%
 9      PERIOD          ANNUAL       QUARTERLY        DAILY    CONTINUOUS
10     ----------------------------------------------------------------
11       50           289.002        369.356        403.031     403.429
12       51           323.682        415.713        454.407     454.865
     ///////////////////// REST OF TABLE NOT SHOWN /////////////////////
```

PART III:
RISK AND RETURN

CHAPTER	TOPIC	NAME	PAGE
9	Stock Risk and Return	BETA	49
10	Portfolio Risk and Return	PORT	53

Part III consists of the two models. A short description of each of the models follows:

BETA - Calculates the risk and return of an asset (generally used for common stock). Returns are one period returns. Risk measures calculated are standard deviation, variance and beta of the asset returns. Both levered and unlevered betas are calculated as is an estimated cost of equity.

PORT - Calculates the risk and return on a portfolio of assets. Input may be either in the form of covariances or correlation coefficients. A detailed view of the calculation is available to the user.

Chapter 9 STOCK RISK AND RETURN

PURPOSE: To calculate the average return, variance and standard deviation of common stock and a market index and the Beta and cost of capital (cost of equity) of common stock. Both Beta and cost of equity are calculated levered and unlevered.

LOADING THE TEMPLATE
From the RISK AND RETURN sub-menu choose number: 1
From LOTUS choose file name: BETA

TEMPLATE MENU: Menu choices available are as follows:
   OLD DATA - input data without erasing existing data
   NEW DATA - erase input data and input new data
   HELP - presents a help screen
   END - allows the user to leave this template

HOW TO INPUT DATA: Choose OLD DATA or NEW DATA menu option. Cursor will move to the first input field. (Note that input fields are generally shown on the screen between ">" and "<" symbols.) Input for this template is in the range of cells C3 - C6 plus C11 to E72, depending upon the number of observations.

EXPLANATION OF CERTAIN INPUTS
   OBS - Number of observations to be input
   t - Corporate tax rate
   B/S - Debt/Equity ratio expressed in market value
   INP - Form of common stock data: 0=Prices; 1=Returns (see additional comments below)

It should be noted that the corporate tax rate, t, and the debt/equity ratio, B/S, are optional inputs. They are not required to run this model.

CAUTION REGARDING INPUT: Two cautions regarding input are in order:

1. The user has the option of entering common stock data in the form of stock prices and dividends or as stock returns. The INP choice (0 or 1) conveys the form to the model for calculation purposes. Market returns (Index Returns) must be entered in return form. **If the user chooses INP = 1, stock returns must be entered in column C, the Stock Price column, in order for calculations to be correct.**

2. The number of observations, OBS, must be correct or an incorrect solution will result. **The number of observations must be equal to the number of paired data points** (stock and index) that are to be entered. OBS will always equal the period number from column A that represents the last entry of both stock and index data.

CALCULATING THE RESULTS
While entering data, press <RET> without entering a number. Calculation will be performed automatically by the program. The program will return to the TEMPLATE MENU after calculation is complete. IMPORTANT: Do not use the LOTUS <F9> key to calculate.

TECHNICAL INFORMATION AND TEMPLATE LIMITATIONS
The template is limited to 60 data observations. Standard linear regression is used to estimate Beta (the coefficient of the X variable where X is market returns and Y is stock returns). This Beta is considered to be a levered Beta, where the leverage is equal to B/S (defined in the input section above). An unlevered Beta (what the Beta would be if the company had no debt) is then estimated from the levered Beta using the following formula:

$$\text{Unlevered Beta} = (\text{Levered Beta})/[1 + (1 - t)*B/S]$$

Levered and unlevered cost of equity estimates are made by using the unlevered and levered beta estimates in the following formula:

$$\text{Levered} = (\text{Market Return} - 8\%) + 8\% * \text{Beta}$$

This last formula assumes that the market commands an 8% risk premium over the risk-free rate.

PROBLEM:
You have gathered the following annual historical common stock prices and dividends for the Happy Daze Company and the corresponding returns on a broad market average:

YEAR	STOCK PRICE	STOCK DIV.	MARKET RETURN
1976	$23.00		
1977	$21.50	$0.75	7.50%
1978	$20.00	$0.80	-1.52%
1979	$22.25	$0.90	14.89%
1980	$24.00	$1.00	9.87%
1981	$25.00	$1.00	6.30%
1982	$27.75	$1.10	14.11%
1983	$31.25	$1.15	11.25%
1984	$34.00	$1.20	13.08%
1985	$34.00	$1.20	-2.28%
1986	$38.75	$1.25	11.96%

Based on this data, a corporate tax rate of 40% and a debt/equity ratio of 25%, determine the average return on the stock, the standard deviation of stock returns, and the levered and unlevered stock Beta.

SOLUTION:

Choose the OLD DATA option and input the following information: OBS = 10, t = .40, B/S = .25 and INP = 0. Enter the data by period. After calculation, the computer screen appears as shown on the next page.

```
<ALT> B to Restart                    STOCK RISK
================================================================
   OBS >          10 < # of Returns (max = 60)
     t >      40.00%< Corporate tax rate                 **************************
   B/S >      25.00%< Debt/Equity (market value)         SOLUTION is based on
   INP >          0 < 0=Prices; 1=Returns                  10 periods of data
  -----------------------------------------------                STOCK       INDEX
                Stock           Index      Stock                -----------------
  Period   Price    Div.       Returns    Returns      AV. RET   9.59%       8.52%
  -----------------------------------------------      STDEV     7.98%       6.12%
    0 >   $23.00    NA           NA <       NA         VAR       0.64%       0.37%
    1 >   $21.50   $0.75        7.50%<    -3.26%       COVARIANCE            0.39%
    2 >   $20.00   $0.80       -1.52%<    -3.26%       CORREL. COEFF.        0.7891
    3 >   $22.25   $0.90       14.89%<    15.75%       R-SQUARED             0.6227
    4 >   $24.00   $1.00        9.87%<    12.36%       -----------------------------
    5 >   $25.00   $1.00        6.30%<     8.33%                LEVERED   UNLEVERED
    6 >   $27.75   $1.10       14.11%<    15.40%                -----------------
    7 >   $31.25   $1.15       11.25%<    16.76%       BETA      1.0292    0.8949
    8 >   $34.00   $1.20       13.08%<    12.64%       k(e)      8.75%     7.68%
    9 >   $34.00   $1.20       -2.28%<     3.53%       **************************
   10 >   $38.75   $1.25       11.96%<    17.64%
```

The solutions as read from the above data are as follows:

Average Return on the Stock	9.59%
Std. Dev. of Stock Returns	7.98%
Levered Beta	1.03
Unlevered Beta	0.89

COMMENT ON SOLUTION

If the user had input all of the above data except for the tax rate and the debt/equity ratio, the solution would have been identical except for the BETA and k(e) [cost of equity]. In this case, the levered and unlevered answers would have shown as identical. That is, the unlevered solutions would have been 1.0292 and 8.75%, respectively.

Chapter 10 PORTFOLIO RISK AND RETURN

PURPOSE: To calculate the expected return, variance and standard deviation of a portfolio of (a maximum of 5) assets.

LOADING THE TEMPLATE
From the RISK AND RETURN sub-menu choose number: 2
From LOTUS choose file name: PORT

TEMPLATE MENU: Menu choices available are as follows:
- OLD DATA - input data without erasing existing data
- NEW DATA - erase input data and input new data
- VIEW - enables the user to view both a variance-covariance and correlation coefficient matrix of asset returns and the detailed calculation of expected portfolio return and risk
- HELP - presents a help screen
- END - allows the user to leave this template

NOTE ABOUT VIEW OPTION: The VIEW menu option provides a view of two screens of data. Screen one shows the variance-covariance matrix and the correlation coefficient matrix. Screen two shows the detailed calculations used to calculate the expected portfolio return and risk. To get from screen one to screen two, **the user must press the <RET> key**. To get from screen two back to the program menu, the <RET> key must be pressed again. The two VIEW screens are shown below for Part I of the SOLUTION.

HOW TO INPUT DATA: Choose OLD DATA or NEW DATA menu option. Cursor will move to the first input field. (Note that input fields are generally shown on the screen between ">" and "<" symbols.) Input for this template is B3 plus cells B8 - E12, depending upon the number of assets (maximum is 5 assets).

EXPLANATION OF CERTAIN INPUTS
- CELL B3 - Input 0 if correlation coefficients are to be used; 1 if covariances used
- RETURNS - Expected asset return for the period
- STD DEV - Standard deviation of the asset returns
- WEIGHT - Percentage that asset represents in portfolio (0-100% acceptable)
- COVARIANCES/CORRELATION COEFFICIENTS - Expresses the relationship of returns between two assets

CAUTION REGARDING INPUTS:
Two cautions are in order.

1. The user must "code" the input correctly in CELL B3.

2. The WEIGHTs of the individual assets must total to 100% or the model will not calculate.

CALCULATING THE RESULTS
While entering data, press <RET> without entering a number. Calculation will be performed automatically by the program. The program will return to the TEMPLATE MENU after calculation is complete. IMPORTANT: Do not use the LOTUS <F9> key to calculate.

TECHNICAL INFORMATION AND TEMPLATE LIMITATIONS
The portfolio is limited to 5 assets.

PROBLEM:
Part I: An investor has the opportunity to invest in two stocks, A and B. The investor has the following expectations regarding the two stocks:

ASSET	RETURNS	STD DEV
A	10.000%	10.000%
B	15.000%	30.000%

If the investor plans to invest equal amounts in each asset and the correlation coefficient between the assets is 1.0 (i.e. perfect correlation), what should the investor expect in terms of a portfolio return and a portfolio standard deviation? Also, given the above information, what is the covariance between assets A and B?

Part II:
Suppose all other facts are as in Part I except that the correlation coefficient between the assets is now 0.4. What will the portfolio return and standard deviation now be?

Chapter 10: Portfolio Risk and Return

SOLUTION:

<u>Part I</u>: Choose OLD DATA or NEW DATA. Input the information provided. The expected return on the portfolio and the expected standard deviation are 12.5% and 20.0%, respectively, as shown below:

```
 1   <ALT> B to Restart            PORTFOLIO RETURNS AND RISK
 2   ================================================================
 3    >       0 < 0 = correlation coefficients; 1 = covariances
 4             ASSET              CORRELATION COEFFICIENTS OR COVARIANCES
 5   ------------------------     ----------------------------------------
 6     RETURNS  STD DEV  WEIGHT         A       B       C       D       E
 7   ------------------------     ----------------------------------------
 8   A>  10.000%  10.000%  50.00% |xxxxxxxx        1
 9   B>  15.000%  30.000%  50.00% |xxxxxxxxxxxxxxxx                              <
10   C>                           |xxxxxxxxxxxxxxxxxxxxxxxx                      <
11   D>                           |xxxxxxxxxxxxxxxxxxxxxxxxxxxxxxxx              <
12   E>                           |xxxxxxxxxxxxxxxxxxxxxxxxxxxxxxxxxxxxxxxx      <
13   ------------------------     ----------------------------------------
14   TOTAL WEIGHT ....... 100.00%
15   ============================ =========================================
16                                        SOLUTION
17   Expected Return on the Portfolio        12.500%
18   Portfolio Variance of Returns            4.000%
19   Portfolio Std. Deviation of Returns     20.000%
20   ================================================================
```

To determine the covariance between the assets, merely select the VIEW menu option and see that the covariance is 0.30. The first screen of the VIEW option shows the following information:

```
21                            ASSET RELATIONSHIPS
22   ---------------------------------------------------------------
23                          VARIANCE/COVARIANCE MATRIX
24            ASSETS     A         B         C         D         E
25          ---------|-----------------------------------------------
26              A      0.010     0.030     0.000     0.000     0.000
27              B      0.030     0.090     0.000     0.000     0.000
28              C      0.000     0.000     0.000     0.000     0.000
29              D      0.000     0.000     0.000     0.000     0.000
30              E      0.000     0.000     0.000     0.000     0.000
31                   ---------------------------------------------
32                          CORRELATION COEFFICIENT MATRIX
33            ASSETS     A         B         C         D         E
34          ---------|-----------------------------------------------
35              A     1.000     1.000       NA        NA        NA
36              B     1.000     1.000       NA        NA        NA
37              C       NA        NA        NA        NA        NA
38              D       NA        NA        NA        NA        NA
39              E       NA        NA        NA        NA        NA
40                   ---------------------------------------------
```

52 Computer Models in Finance

Although not required in the solution to this particular problem, the second screen of the VIEW option shows the detailed calculations made to determine the portfolio return and risk. This second screen, reached by pressing <RET> from the above screen, appears below:

```
21                        ASSET RELATIONSHIPS
22    ------------------------------------------------------------
41        Return   Weight  Extend  ////////
42    A>  10.00%   50.00%   5.00%  ////////
43    B>  15.00%   50.00%   7.50%  //////// DETAILED RETURN CALCULATION
44    C>   0.00%    0.00%   0.00%  ////////
45    D>   0.00%    0.00%   0.00%  ////////
46    E>   0.00%    0.00%   0.00%  ////////
47    ---------------------------  ////////
48        Portfolio Return  12.50%
49    ============================================================
50         A        B        C        D        E     Total  //////
51    A> 0.250%   0.750%   0.000%   0.000%   0.000%  1.000% //////
52    B> 0.750%   2.250%   0.000%   0.000%   0.000%  3.000% ////// DETAILED
53    C> 0.000%   0.000%   0.000%   0.000%   0.000%  0.000% ////// VARIANCE
54    D> 0.000%   0.000%   0.000%   0.000%   0.000%  0.000% ////// CALC.
55    E> 0.000%   0.000%   0.000%   0.000%   0.000%  0.000% //////
56    ------------------------------------------------------- //////
57                 Portfolio Variance          4.000%
58    ============================================================
```

Part II:
Select OLD DATA and merely change the correlation coefficient to 0.4. The results are as follows:

```
    Expected Return on the Portfolio          12.500%
    Portfolio Variance of Returns              3.100%
    Portfolio Std. Deviation of Returns       17.607%
```

PART IV:
VALUATION

CHAPTER	TOPIC	NAME	PAGE
11	Bonds	BOND	59
12	Mortgages	MORT	63
13	Leases	LEASE	69
14	Preferred Stock	PREFER	71
15	Common Stock	STOCK	73

Part IV presents valuation models for five common financial instruments. A brief description of each model follows:

BOND - Solves for either the market value or yield-to-maturity of conventional and/or zero-coupon bonds.

MORT - Generates mortgage amortization tables

LEASE - Solves for the present value of a stream of lease payments. The present value of the entire stream and that portion to be capitalized for accounting purposes are both calculated.

PREFER - Calculates market value, interest rate or dividend of preferred stock

STOCK - Calculates the market value of common stock based on expected dividends. An irregular dividend pattern for up to 10 periods can be used. A constant-growth-to-infinity dividend stream is employed.

Chapter 11 BONDS

PURPOSE: To calculate market value or yield-to-maturity of conventional and zero-coupon bonds.

LOADING THE TEMPLATE
From the VALUATION sub-menu choose number: 1
From LOTUS choose file name: BOND

TEMPLATE MENU: Menu choices available are as follows:
   DATA - input data
   VIEW - enables user to view sensitivity analysis
   GRAPH - shows sensitivity analysis in graph form
   END - allows the user to leave this template

HOW TO INPUT DATA: Choose DATA menu option. Cursor will move to the first input field. (Note that input fields are generally shown on the screen between ">" and "<" symbols.) Input for this template is in the range of cells C8 - C14.

EXPLANATION OF CERTAIN INPUTS
   Unknown - Enter number of unknown variable: PV = 1; k(d) = 2
       Note that PV is equivalent to market value and k(d) is yield-to-maturity (or IRR).
   PV - Current market value of the bond
   k(d) - Required rate of return on the bond
   Coupon r - Annual coupon interest on the bond (0 for zero-coupon bonds)
   Face - Face value of bond (amount paid upon maturity)
   Term - Number of years to maturity
   Int/yr - Number of interest payments per year

CALCULATING THE RESULTS
While entering data, press <RET> without entering a number. Calculation will be performed automatically by the program. The program will return to the TEMPLATE MENU after calculation is complete. IMPORTANT: Do not use the LOTUS <F9> key to calculate.

TECHNICAL INFORMATION AND TEMPLATE LIMITATIONS
Only current market value (PV) or yield-to-maturity (Effective Interest) can be calculated. All cash flows are assumed to occur at the end of the period. The number of years to maturity (Term) must be in full years. Yield-to-maturity will show as ERR if the IRR algorithm fails to converge.

PROBLEMS:
Solve the following:

PROBLEM 1: A bond pays 10% per year in equal semi-annual payments. If it has a face value of $10,000, matures in 5 years and require a return of 12% by market participants, what will its price be (i.e. what is the present value)?

PROBLEM 2: A bond sells for $65 with a coupon rate of 5 percent paid semi-annually, a face value of $100.00 and a maturity 15 years from now. What is the effective yield to maturity on this bond?

PROBLEM 3: A zero-coupon bond matures in 5 years and pays $1,000 at that time. If an 11% return is required on the bond, how much should the bond sell for?

SOLUTIONS

PROBLEM 1.
Choose the DATA option and input the following information: Unknown = 1; k(d) = .12; Coupon r = .10; Face = 10000; Term = 5; Int/yr = 2. The answer, shown in the upper right-hand corner of the screen, is $9,263.99. The screen appears as follows:

```
===================================================================
                                                        SOLUTION
                        ===========================================
                                    MARKET VALUE =     $9,263.99
                INPUTS               YLD-TO-MAT.  =         NA
-------------------------------------------------------------------
Unknown    >             1 <    Enter number to solve for: PV=1; k(d)=2
PV         >               <    Market Value of Bond
k(d)       >        12.00%<     Req'd Ret (yield to maturity)
Coupon r   >        10.00%<     Coupon Interest Rate (annual)
Face       >      $10,000 <     Face Value of Bond
Term       >             5 <    Years to Maturity
Int./yr    >             2 <    Number of Interest Payments per Year
-------------------------------------------------------------------
```

PROBLEM 2.
Choose the DATA option and input the relevant information. The solution is 9.399%, and the screen should appear as follows:

```
================================================================
                                                    SOLUTION
                                  ==============================
                          MARKET VALUE =           NA
              INPUTS      YLD-TO-MAT.  =        9.399%
----------------------------------------------------------------
Unknown   >         2 <   Enter number to solve for: PV=1; k(d)=2
PV        >    $65.00 <   Market Value of Bond
k(d)      >           <   Req'd Ret (yield to maturity)
Coupon r  >     5.00%<    Coupon Interest Rate (annual)
Face      >      $100 <   Face Value of Bond
Term      >        15 <   Years to Maturity
Int./yr   >         2 <   Number of Interest Payments per Year
----------------------------------------------------------------
```

PROBLEM 3.
Choose the DATA option and input the following: Unknown = 1; k(d) = .11; Coupon r = 0; Face = 1000; Term = 5. Make sure that all other input items are zero or blank. The answer is $593.45 as shown below:

```
================================================================
                                                    SOLUTION
                                  ==============================
                          MARKET VALUE =         $593.45
              INPUTS      YLD-TO-MAT.  =           NA
----------------------------------------------------------------
Unknown   >         1 <   Enter number to solve for: PV=1; k(d)=2
PV        >           <   Market Value of Bond
k(d)      >    11.00%<    Req'd Ret (yield to maturity)
Coupon r  >     0.00%<    Coupon Interest Rate (annual)
Face      >    $1,000 <   Face Value of Bond
Term      >         5 <   Years to Maturity
Int./yr   >         0 <   Number of Interest Payments per Year
----------------------------------------------------------------
```

Chapter 12 MORTGAGES

PURPOSE: To calculate mortgage amortization tables.

LOADING THE TEMPLATE
From the VALUATION sub-menu choose number: 2
From LOTUS choose file name: MORT

TEMPLATE MENU: Menu choices available are as follows:
   DATA - input data
   VIEW - view the amortization table
   GRAPH - view graph of interest and principal
   PRINT - print the amortization table
   HELP - view help screen
   END - allows the user to leave this template

HOW TO INPUT DATA: Choose DATA menu option. Cursor will move to the first input field. (Note that input fields are generally shown on the screen between ">" and "<" symbols.) Input for this template is in the range of cells from C3 - C8.

EXPLANATION OF CERTAIN INPUTS
   Mortgage - Amount borrowed
   Int. Rate - Annual interest rate (as a decimal)
   Years - Length of mortgage in years
   Balloon - Amount of balloon payment (if any) in last period
   Times Paid - The number of payments made per year
   Period - First time period shown in amortization table. This
         entry is usually 1 but can be raised to see later years
         in a long-term mortgage.

CALCULATING THE RESULTS
While entering data, press <RET> without entering a number. Calculation will be performed automatically by the program. The program will return to the TEMPLATE MENU after calculation is complete. IMPORTANT: Do not use the LOTUS <F9> key to calculate.

TECHNICAL INFORMATION AND TEMPLATE LIMITATIONS

Any balloon payment is in addition to the level regular payments.

The amortization table only handles 36 periods at once. This limitation may be obviated by increasing the Period input to deal with latter periods.

PROBLEM:

PART I:

John Jones wants to obtain a $50,000 mortgage for a new home. He thinks that he can obtain one for 25 years at 12% interest.
    (A) What will his monthly payment be?
    (B) How much will he still owe after 5 years?
    (C) How much will the monthly payments be if John obtains a 15 year mortgage (all other information the same)?
    (D) How much will he owe with a 15 year mortgage after 5 years?

PART II:

Mary Jones, John's sister, is a real estate tycoon. She needs a $50,000 mortgage for a project she wishes to purchase. The bank offers her a 15 year mortgage at 12% interest. From John (Part C above) she knows that the monthly payments will be $600.08 per month. Unfortunately this amount is too much for the project to support. Mary believes that based on past experience with this bank, they will allow her to pay down on only $30,000 of the $50,000 and make a balloon payment in the fifteenth year. (Mary would, of course, have to pay monthly interest on the $20,000). If she can achieve such a loan, what will her monthly payments be, and what will she owe after five years?

SOLUTION:

Part I (A):
Choose the DATA option and input the given information. The solution is $526.61 per month. The input and the 36 months of output appear on the next page.

```
 1  <ALT> B to Restart          MORTGAGE AMORTIZATION
 2  ================================================================
 3  Mortgage      >      $50,000 < Amount borrowed (Principal)
 4  Int. Rate     >       12.00%< Annual Interest Rate - %
 5  Years         >           25 < Years until paid off
 6  Balloon       >           $0 < Last payment, if different than others
 7  Times Paid    >           12 < Payments per year (e.g. 12=monthly)
 8  Period        >            1 < First period to show below
 9  ----------------------------------------------------------------
10  PRINCIPAL =          $50,000            25 YEARS        AT           12.00%
11     12 PAYMENTS/YR                       $0 BALLOON PAYMENT
12  ----------------------------------------------------------------
13  Period             Payment       Interest      Principal    End. Balance
14  ================================================================
15     1               $526.61        $500.00         $26.61      $49,973.39
16     2               $526.61        $499.73         $26.88      $49,946.51
17     3               $526.61        $499.47         $27.15      $49,919.36
18     4               $526.61        $499.19         $27.42      $49,891.94
19     5               $526.61        $498.92         $27.69      $49,864.25
20     6               $526.61        $498.64         $27.97      $49,836.28
21     7               $526.61        $498.36         $28.25      $49,808.03
22     8               $526.61        $498.08         $28.53      $49,779.50
23     9               $526.61        $497.80         $28.82      $49,750.68
24    10               $526.61        $497.51         $29.11      $49,721.58
////////////  SOME DATA EXCLUDED FOR SPACE CONSIDERATIONS  ////////////
31    17               $526.61        $495.41         $31.20      $49,509.53
32    18               $526.61        $495.10         $31.52      $49,478.01
33    19               $526.61        $494.78         $31.83      $49,446.18
34    20               $526.61        $494.46         $32.15      $49,414.03
35    21               $526.61        $494.14         $32.47      $49,381.56
36    22               $526.61        $493.82         $32.80      $49,348.76
37    23               $526.61        $493.49         $33.12      $49,315.64
38    24               $526.61        $493.16         $33.46      $49,282.18
39    25               $526.61        $492.82         $33.79      $49,248.39
40    26               $526.61        $492.48         $34.13      $49,214.26
41    27               $526.61        $492.14         $34.47      $49,179.79
42    28               $526.61        $491.80         $34.81      $49,144.98
43    29               $526.61        $491.45         $35.16      $49,109.82
44    30               $526.61        $491.10         $35.51      $49,074.30
45    31               $526.61        $490.74         $35.87      $49,038.43
46    32               $526.61        $490.38         $36.23      $49,002.21
47    33               $526.61        $490.02         $36.59      $48,965.62
48    34               $526.61        $489.66         $36.96      $48,928.66
49    35               $526.61        $489.29         $37.33      $48,891.33
50    36               $526.61        $488.91         $37.70      $48,853.64
51  ----------------------------------------------------------------
52  TOTALS          $18,958.03     $17,811.67      $1,146.36
53  ================================================================
```

Part I (B):
Choose DATA option. Change Period to 60. Solution is $47,826.60 remaining after five years (60 months):

```
 1   <ALT> B to Restart         MORTGAGE AMORTIZATION
 2   ================================================================
 3   Mortgage     >      $50,000 < Amount borrowed (Principal)
 4   Int. Rate    >       12.00%< Annual Interest Rate - %
 5   Years        >           25 < Years until paid off
 6   Balloon      >           $0 < Last payment, if different than others
 7   Times Paid   >           12 < Payments per year (e.g. 12=monthly)
 8   Period       >           60 < First period to show below
 9   ----------------------------------------------------------------
10   PRINCIPAL =       $50,000           25 YEARS      AT         12.00%
11      12 PAYMENTS/YR                   $0 BALLOON PAYMENT
12   ----------------------------------------------------------------
13   Period            Payment      Interest     Principal    End. Balance
14   ================================================================
15       60            $526.61      $478.74       $47.87       $47,826.60
16       61            $526.61      $478.27       $48.35       $47,778.25
//////////////////////////////////////////////////////////
```

PART I (C) and PART I (D):
Choose Data option. Change Years to 15. Solution to (C) is $600.08 per month and to (D) is $41,826.17. (NOTE that you do not have to change the Period back to 1 because all monthly payments are the same). The solution appears below:

```
 1   <ALT> B to Restart         MORTGAGE AMORTIZATION
 2   ================================================================
 3   Mortgage     >      $50,000 < Amount borrowed (Principal)
 4   Int. Rate    >       12.00%< Annual Interest Rate - %
 5   Years        >           15 < Years until paid off
 6   Balloon      >           $0 < Last payment, if different than others
 7   Times Paid   >           12 < Payments per year (e.g. 12=monthly)
 8   Period       >           60 < First period to show below
 9   ----------------------------------------------------------------
10   PRINCIPAL =       $50,000           15 YEARS      AT         12.00%
11      12 PAYMENTS/YR                   $0 BALLOON PAYMENT
12   ----------------------------------------------------------------
13   Period            Payment      Interest     Principal    End. Balance
14   ================================================================
15       60            $600.08      $420.06      $180.02       $41,826.17
16       61            $600.08      $418.26      $181.82       $41,644.35
//////////////////////////////////////////////////////////
```

PART II:

Choose DATA option, and input the information as shown below. The monthly payments are reduced to $560.05. However the amount owed after five years is higher: $45,095.70.

```
 1   <ALT> B to Restart         MORTGAGE AMORTIZATION
 2   ================================================================
 3   Mortgage    >      $50,000 < Amount borrowed (Principal)
 4   Int. Rate   >       12.00%< Annual Interest Rate - %
 5   Years       >           15 < Years until paid off
 6   Balloon     >      $20,000 < Last payment, if different than others
 7   Times Paid  >           12 < Payments per year (e.g. 12=monthly)
 8   Period      >           60 < First period to show below
 9   ----------------------------------------------------------------
10   PRINCIPAL =        $50,000           15 YEARS      AT      12.00%
11      12 PAYMENTS/YR            $20,000 BALLOON PAYMENT
12   ----------------------------------------------------------------
13   Period          Payment     Interest   Principal   End. Balance
14   ================================================================
15      60           $560.05     $452.04    $108.01     $45,095.70
16      61           $560.05     $450.96    $109.09     $44,986.61
////////////////////////////////////////////////////////////////////
```

Chapter 13 LEASES

PURPOSE: To calculate the present value of a lease. Calculations include amount to be capitalized for accounting purposes and the amount that shows as a current liability.

LOADING THE TEMPLATE
From the VALUATION sub-menu choose number: 3
From LOTUS choose file name: LEASE

TEMPLATE MENU: Menu choices available are as follows:
   DATA - input data
   HELP - presents a help screen
   END - allows the user to leave this template

HOW TO INPUT DATA: Choose DATA menu option. Cursor will move to the first input field. (Note that input fields are generally shown on the screen between ">" and "<" symbols.) Input for this template is in the range of cells C3 - C7.

EXPLANATION OF CERTAIN INPUTS
   Payments per Year - Number of lease payments per year (must be
      number equal to or greater than one
   Payment Amount - Amount of each lease payment
   Payments Remaining - Number of lease payments yet to be made
   Land % - Estimated value of leased land as a percentage of
      estimated value of total leased assets
   Annual Disc. Rate - Interest rate applicable to lease for
      present value purposes

CALCULATING THE RESULTS
While entering data, press <RET> without entering a number. Calculation will be performed automatically by the program. The program will return to the TEMPLATE MENU after calculation is complete. IMPORTANT: Do not use the LOTUS <F9> key to calculate.

TECHNICAL INFORMATION AND TEMPLATE LIMITATIONS
The present value calculations assume that the next payment is due immediately. That is, the first of the remaining lease payments is assumed to occur at time period 0.

PROBLEM:
ABC Company leases a building for $1,000 per month. There are 60 monthly lease payments remaining, the relevant discount rate is 12%, and the company estimates that the land value is about 10% of the total leased asset value. What is the present value of the remaining lease payments, and how much would be capitalized according to generally accepted accounting principles?

SOLUTION:
Choose the DATA option and enter the given information. After calculation, the screen should appear as shown below. The answers are $45,404.59 for present value of the total lease and $40,864.13 for the portion that would be capitalized.

```
1   <ALT> B to Restart                LEASE VALUATION
2   ================================================================
3   Payments per Year   >          12   < 12=Monthly; 4=Quarterly; 1=Annually
4   Payment Amount      >     1000.00   < Amount of Each Payment
5   Payments Remaining  >          60   < Number of payments to be made
6   Land %              >       10.00%  < Percentage of Lease not Capitalized
7   Annual Disc. Rate   >       12.00%  < Interest rate applicable to lease
8   ----------------------------------------------------------------
9                                                  SENSITIVITY ANALYSIS
10            SOLUTION:                             11.00%       13.00%
11  =================================================  ---------------------
12  PRESENT VAL. OF TOTAL LEASE        $45,404.59   $46,414.64  $44,426.23
13  =================================================  =====================
14          ACCOUNTING INFORMATION:                 ACCOUNTING INFORMATION:
15  -------------------------------------------------  ---------------------
16  CAPITALIZED LEASE                  $40,864.13   $41,773.17  $39,983.61
17  CURRENT LIABILITY                   $5,787.57    $6,696.61   $4,907.05
18  INTEREST NEXT 12 MONTHS             $5,012.43    $4,103.39   $5,892.95
19  ================================================================
```

Chapter 14 PREFERRED STOCK

PURPOSE: To calculate market value, interest rate or dividend of preferred stock. (Compare this model with the Perpetuities model, PERPETUY, in Chapter 6.)

LOADING THE TEMPLATE
From the VALUATION sub-menu choose number: 4
From LOTUS choose file name: PREFER

TEMPLATE MENU: Menu choices available are as follows:
   DATA - input data
   HELP - presents a help screen
   END - allows the user to leave this template

HOW TO INPUT DATA: Choose DATA menu option. Cursor will move to the first input field. (Note that input fields are generally shown on the screen between ">" and "<" symbols.) Input for this template is in the range of cells C8 - C11.

EXPLANATION OF CERTAIN INPUTS
   UNKNOWN - Enter number of unknown variable: price = 1; Div = 2; r = 3
   r - Interest rate or required return (as a decimal)
   pv - Current market value of the preferred stock
   Div - Dividend per share

CALCULATING THE RESULTS
While entering data, press <RET> without entering a number. Calculation will be performed automatically by the program. The program will return to the TEMPLATE MENU after calculation is complete. IMPORTANT: Do not use the LOTUS <F9> key to calculate.

TECHNICAL INFORMATION AND TEMPLATE LIMITATIONS
The formula used in the preferred stock calculations is a version of the perpetuity formula:

$$PV = Div/r$$

where the terms are defined as above.

PROBLEMS:

PROBLEM 1 : What is the price of a preferred stock which pays a dividend of $45.00 per share per year and requires a return of 12.5%?

PROBLEM 2 : What is the effective yield on a preferred stock which sells for $120.00 and pays a dividend of $20.00 annually?

PROBLEM 3 : If a preferred stock requires an 11% return and sells for $120.00, what must its dividend be?

68 Computer Models in Finance

SOLUTIONS:

PROBLEM 1.

Choose the DATA option and input the following information: Unknown = 1; r = .125 and Div = 45. The answer as shown in the upper-right corner is $360.00:

```
 2 ================================================================
 3                                   ***********   SOLUTION   ********
 4                                   PRESENT VALUE =          $360.00
 5                                   EFF. INTEREST =               NA
 6                         INPUT:    ************************************
 7 ----------------------------------------------------------------
 8 UNKNOWN  >                   1 <  Unknown Variable (1=Price, 2=Div, 3=r)
 9 r        >              12.50%<   Required Rate of Return (%)
10 pv       >                    <   Price
11 Div      >              $45.00 <  Dividend (annual, per share)
12 ----------------------------------------------------------------
```

PROBLEM 2.

```
 2 ================================================================
 3                                   ***********   SOLUTION   ********
 4                                   PRESENT VALUE =               NA
 5                                   EFF. INTEREST =           16.67%
 6                         INPUT:    ************************************
 7 ----------------------------------------------------------------
 8 UNKNOWN  >                   3 <  Unknown Variable (1=Price, 2=Div, 3=r)
 9 r        >                    <   Required Rate of Return (%)
10 pv       >             $120.00 <  Price
11 Div      >              $20.00 <  Dividend (annual, per share)
12 ----------------------------------------------------------------
```

PROBLEM 3.

```
 2 ================================================================
 3                                   ***********   SOLUTION   ********
 4                                   DIVIDEND                  $13.20
 5                                   EFF. INTEREST =               NA
 6                         INPUT:    ************************************
 7 ----------------------------------------------------------------
 8 UNKNOWN  >                   2 <  Unknown Variable (1=Price, 2=Div, 3=r)
 9 r        >              11.00% <  Required Rate of Return (%)
10 pv       >             $120.00 <  Price
11 Div      >                    <   Dividend (annual, per share)
12 ----------------------------------------------------------------
```

Chapter 15 COMMON STOCK

PURPOSE To calculate the market value of common stock based on expected dividends. An irregular dividend pattern for up to 10 periods can be used. A constant-growth-to-infinity dividend stream is employed.

LOADING THE TEMPLATE
From the VALUATION sub-menu choose number: 5
From LOTUS choose file name: STOCK

TEMPLATE MENU Menu choices available and their functions are as follows:
   DATA - input data
   GRAPH - output shown in graph form
   VIEW - enables user to view sensitivity analysis
   HELP - presents a help screen
   END - allows the user to leave this template

HOW TO INPUT DATA
Choose DATA option from menu. Cursor will move to the first input field. (Note that input fields are generally shown on the screen between ">" and "<" symbols.) Input for this template is in the range of cells C3 - C19 excluding cells C4, C5 and C17.

EXPLANATION OF CERTAIN INPUTS
k(e) - Required rate of return on the stock (in decimal form)
DIV for time periods 0 thru 10 - Expected dividends per share
   (all periods need not be input)
g - Constant growth to infinity
Yr. - Year of first dividend reflecting constant growth (must be
   value 1 - 11) (See INPUT CAUTION below for example.)

INPUT CAUTION
Individual dividends entered in years 1 - 10 may be superseded by constant growth input. All individual dividends occurring after the first constant growth dividend are superseded and ignored in the calculations. For example, if the first constant growth dividend occurs in year 6, any individual dividends entered years in 6-10 will be superseded and not calculated in the PRESENT VALUE OF DIVIDEND column.

CALCULATING THE RESULTS
While entering data, press <RET> without entering a number. Calculation will be performed automatically by the program. The program will return to the TEMPLATE MENU after calculation is complete. IMPORTANT: Do not use the LOTUS <F9> key to calculate.

VIEW and GRAPH
Both these options provide looks at the sensitivity of the common stock price to a range of different required returns and constant growth rates to infinity. The pattern of the first ten years of dividends is assumed in these calculations.

TECHNICAL INFORMATION AND TEMPLATE LIMITATIONS
All dividends are assumed to occur at the end of the time period. The first constant growth dividend must occur no earlier than year 1 and no later than the 11th year. The rate of constant growth [g] must be smaller than the required rate of return on the stock [k(e)].

PROBLEMS

PROBLEM 1:
Alfred Bozo, stock market analyst for the Acme Brokerage Company, is attempting to value the Weasel Coat Company's common stock. He expects Weasel to increase its dividend by 5% per year for as far out as he can estimate. The next dividend is to be paid a year from now and is estimated at $1.25 per share. If the market requires a 14% return on this stock, what should Bozo estimate for the price of the common stock?

PROBLEM 2:
Joe Hardworker, analyst for the Bith Smarney Co., also is trying to value the Weasel Coat Company's common stock. His estimates differ somewhat from Mr. Bozo's. Specifically, he believes the company will increase its dividends by 15% per year for the next three years (years 2-4). Thereafter he believes the company can increase its dividend by 6% per year forever. If he estimates the next dividend at $1.25 and a required rate of return of 15%, what value will he place on the stock?

SOLUTIONS

PROBLEM 1:
Choose the DATA option. Input .14 for k(e), 1.25 in time period 1 and .05 for g and 2 for Yr. The answer is $13.89 and the screen should appear as follows:

```
                       COMMON STOCK VALUATION
================================================================
k(e) >        14%<    VALUE OF CONSTANT        PRESENT VALUE OF
YEAR****     DIV. <     GROWTH         DIVIDEND      GROWTH
----------------------------------------------------------------
   0 >             <    $0.00           $0.00         $0.00
   1 >     $1.25   <   $14.58           $1.10        $12.79
   2 >             <    $0.00           $0.00         $0.00
   3 >             <    $0.00           $0.00         $0.00
   4 >             <    $0.00           $0.00         $0.00
   5 >             <    $0.00           $0.00         $0.00
   6 >             <    $0.00           $0.00         $0.00
   7 >             <    $0.00           $0.00         $0.00
   8 >             <    $0.00           $0.00         $0.00
   9 >             <    $0.00           $0.00         $0.00
  10 >             <    $0.00           $0.00         $0.00
****GROWTH****     <                   =======================
   g >         5%<   Constant Growth Rat$1.10 TOTAL    $12.79
  Yr. >        2 <   Yr of Growth Div. (    MARKET VA  $13.89
----------------------------------------------------------------
```

PROBLEM 2:

Choose the DATA option and input the information provided above.
(See COMMENT below for input advice, especially if you have
trouble obtaining the correct answer.) The correct solution
(shown in lower-right-hand portion of the screen) is $17.15.
After input and calculation, the screen should appear as follows:

```
                    COMMON STOCK VALUATION
===============================================================
k(e)>          15%<    VALUE OF CONSTANT       PRESENT VALUE OF
YEAR****       DIV. <    GROWTH       DIVIDEND      GROWTH
---------------------------------------------------------------
   0 >              <    $0.00         $0.00        $0.00
   1 >     $1.25 <       $0.00         $1.09        $0.00
   2 >     $1.44 <       $0.00         $1.09        $0.00
   3 >     $1.65 <       $0.00         $1.09        $0.00
   4 >     $1.90 <      $22.39         $1.09       $12.80
   5 >           <       $0.00         $0.00        $0.00
   6 >           <       $0.00         $0.00        $0.00
   7 >           <       $0.00         $0.00        $0.00
   8 >           <       $0.00         $0.00        $0.00
   9 >           <       $0.00         $0.00        $0.00
  10 >           <       $0.00         $0.00        $0.00
****GROWTH****  <                 ======================
   g >       6%<   Constant Growth Rat$4.35 TOTAL   $12.80
  Yr. >       5 <  Yr of Growth Div. (    MARKET VA  $17.15
---------------------------------------------------------------
```

COMMENT ON PROBLEM 2
The method in which the dividends are input will influence the
answer you obtain. Two approaches of input are apt to be chosen:
(a) input 1.25*1.15, 1.44*1.15 etc. or (b) input 1.25*1.15,
+C7*1.15, etc. Approaches (a) and (b) will produce slightly different results due to the rounding involved. Approach (a) rounds
off to two significant decimal places. Approach (b) will account
properly for the fractional dividends because, even though the
numbers are only shown to two decimal places, LOTUS stores them
with substantial precision. This author used approach (b) to obtain the results shown above. If you use an approach similar to
(a), you will be off by some small amount (probably only pennies
in this particular problem).

The difference in answers provided by the two different approaches is usually not significant. This statement is especially true when one considers the error factor inherent in forecasting future dividends. The reason to point these differences out
is to minimize the confusion that might result when the computer
"gives me the wrong answer."

PART V:
STATEMENT ANALYSIS

CHAPTER	TOPIC	NAME	PAGE
16	Overview of Financial Analysis	/not model/	79
17	Financial Statements	FINSTATE	83
18	Ratio Analysis	RATIO	93
19	Common Size Analysis	COMSIZE	97
20	Changes in Fin'l Position	FUNDSFLO	101
21	Pro Forma Statements	PLAN	102

Part V deals with the analysis of financial statements. This section can be especially useful to anyone concerned with credit analysis, fundamental analysis for investment purposes, evaluation of company performance and a host of other purposes. Students should find it quite useful in the analysis of cases.

There are six chapters in this section and five models. Chapter 16 does not deal with a model but presents an overview of the software relationships between the models. Chapter 17 (FINSTATE) is an important chapter and model because all other models in this section depend upon this particular model.

Prior to using any of the models in this section, it is important that users read and understand Chapters 16 and 17.

A brief description of the models follows:

FINSTATE - model to prepare and save financial statements
RATIO - ratio analysis of financial statements
COMSIZE - common size (or index) analysis
FUNDSFLO - statement of changes in financial position
PLAN - three-year forecast of financial statements

Chapter 16 OVERVIEW OF FINANCIAL STATEMENTS

PURPOSE
This chapter is unique in that it does not deal directly with a particular financial model. Rather it provides an overview of the models that follow in the next five chapters. The overview focuses on software relationships <u>only</u>.

UNDERSTANDING MODELS VERSUS UNDERSTANDING ANALYSIS
It is important to understand these models in order to operate them properly on your computer. However, understanding the models is not the same as understanding how to perform financial analysis. **Effective analysis is produced by an analyst and not by computer models.** Models merely reduce the amount of calculation required. They are no substitute for thinking.

> **Learning how to use these models is not sufficient for producing effective financial analysis.**

A thorough understanding of the financial concepts involved in ratio analysis, common size analysis, statement of changes in financial position and pro forma statements is a requisite for anyone performing statement analysis. A focus on the financial relationships of the tools in this section is beyond the scope of this chapter or book.

> **Students should consult their financial text for these relationships.**

KEY RELATIONSHIP
Performing financial analysis using these models involves two general steps:

1. Financial Statement Preparation
2. Financial Statement Analysis

One model (FINSTATE) allows a user to create financial statements. Four models (RATIO, COMSIZE, FUNDSFLO, PLAN) perform analysis on financial statements.

> **All analysis performed by RATIO, COMSIZE, FUNDSFLO or PLAN must be done on statements that were prepared using FINSTATE.**

FINSTATE provides the input data for the other models in this section. **No financial data can be entered directly (via the computer keyboard) into any of these models except FINSTATE.** Files prepared using the FINSTATE model are the input for the other models.

FINANCIAL STATEMENT PREPARATION
To prepare financial statements, do the following:

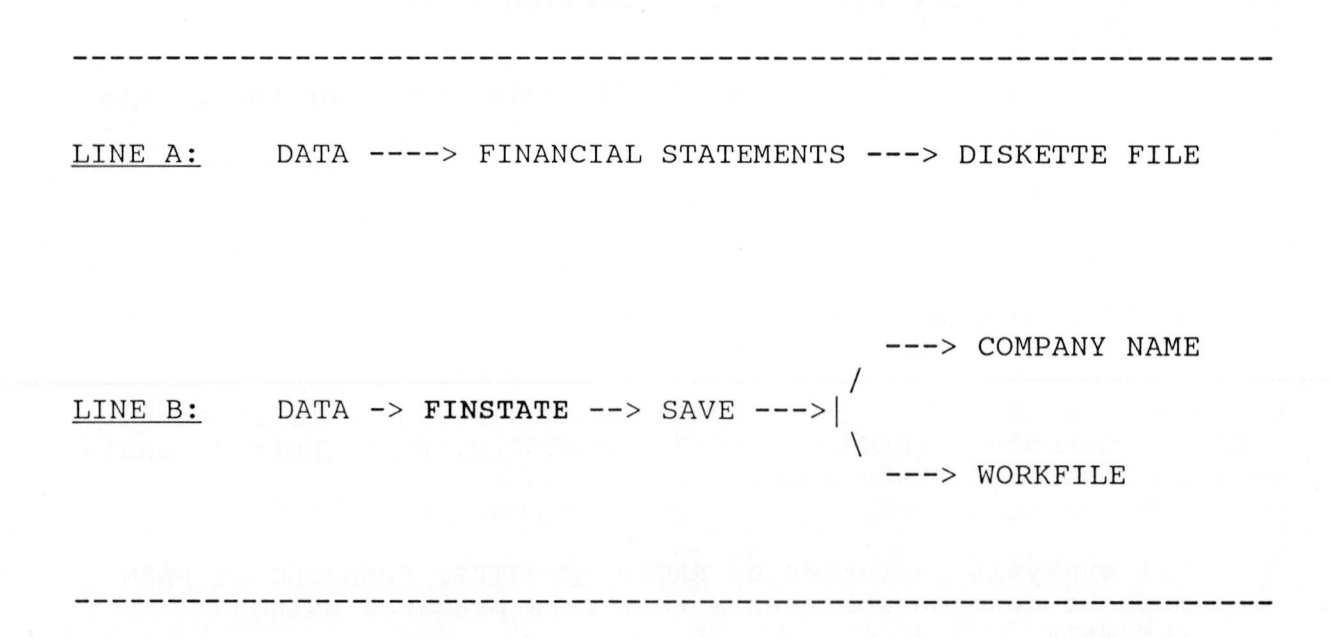

1. Load FINSTATE
2. Enter financial data via the keyboard
3. Save financial data to a file on a diskette

The data is saved to diskette under the company name or as "WORK-FILE" (see next chapter for more detail on the saved files). Graphically, Exhibit XVI-1 represents the steps in financial statement preparation. Line A shows the generic steps involved, while line B shows the steps using the models.

EXHIBIT XVI-1

FINANCIAL STATEMENT PREPARATION

LINE A: DATA ----> FINANCIAL STATEMENTS ---> DISKETTE FILE

                                          ---> COMPANY NAME
                                         /
LINE B: DATA -> **FINSTATE** --> SAVE --->|
                                         \
                                          ---> WORKFILE

FINANCIAL STATEMENT ANALYSIS

To analyze financial statements, do the following:

1. Load model (RATIO, COMSIZE, FUNDSFLO or PLAN)
2. Retrieve financial statements from diskette

In graphic form, the process is shown in Exhibit XVI-2. Part A is the generic representation while Part B shows the analysis models.

EXHIBIT XVI-2

ANALYSIS OF DATA

PART A:

FINANCIAL STATEMENTS ---> ANALYSIS MODEL

PART B:

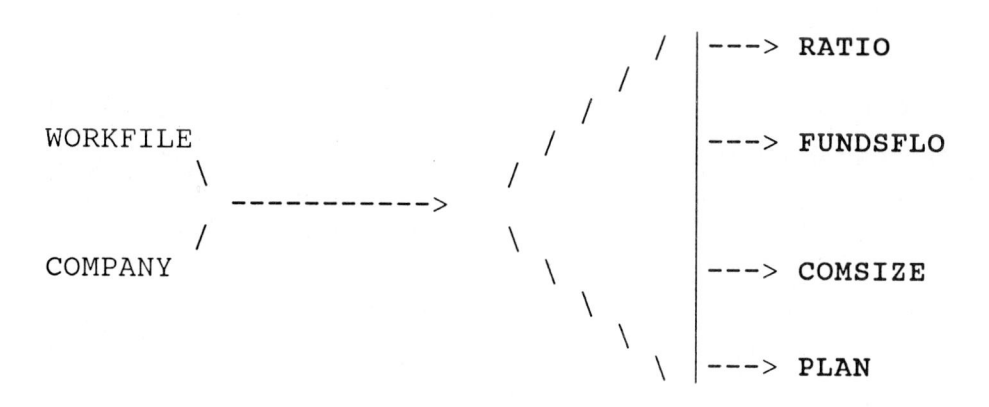

```
                                    /  |---> RATIO
                                   /   |
                                  /    |
WORKFILE                         /     |---> FUNDSFLO
         \    ----------->      \      |
         /                       \     |
COMPANY                           \    |---> COMSIZE
                                   \   |
                                    \  |---> PLAN
```

Financial analysis is automatically performed when the statements are brought into the particular model. Consult the following chapters for more detailed information on particular models.

HOW TO PERFORM A COMPLETE FINANCIAL ANALYSIS ON A COMPANY
It is rather easy to develop all of the data on a particular company. The following outline shows the steps that should be performed:

1. Load FINSTATE and enter data. Save data to WORKFILE (you may also wish to save it to a file under the company name).

2. Load RATIO and import WORKFILE. Print out analysis.

3. Load COMSIZE and import WORKFILE. Print out analysis.

4. Load FUNDSFLO and import WORKFILE. Print out analysis.

5. Load PLAN and import WORKFILE. Make modifications, if needed. CALC until convergence. Print out analysis.

Although this summary precedes the detail on the particular models, it conveys how simple it is to use these models together. After reading the individual chapters, this particular section can provide a good reference when you want to completely analyze a company.

USE OF GRAPHS
For those users who have the hardware capabilities of using the GRAPH menu options, it is especially recommended that these options be explored for statement analysis. Relationships that are difficult to spot when looking at a page of numbers, often are easier to comprehend in graph form.

Once again, you may view graphs on the screen but not print them to a printer.

Chapter 17 FINANCIAL STATEMENTS

PURPOSE: To provide a standard format for financial statements, a means of storing financial data and an input module for the financial analysis models.

LOADING THE TEMPLATE
From the STATEMENT ANALYSIS sub-menu choose number: 1
From LOTUS choose file name: FINSTATE

TEMPLATE MENU
Menu choices available and their functions are as follows:
  OLD DATA - input data via overtyping existing data
  NEW DATA - erase existing data and input new data
  PRINT - prints income statement and balance sheet
  SAVE - saves financial statements
  HELP - presents a help screen
  END - allows the user to leave this template

VIEW is not available as a menu option. To view the data in the financial statements, choose OLD DATA option and then NUMBERS and merely move around the spreadsheet without entering a number. (See DATA MODIFICATION OR ADDITION ALLOWED section on the next page for related information.)

HOW TO INPUT DATA
Choose OLD DATA or NEW DATA menu option. When you first load the template, either choice will result in the NEW DATA sub-menu. If data has already been entered into the template and you subsequently choose to input data, OLD DATA and NEW DATA choices will differ. The table below summarizes these choices with and without data already in the template:

EFFECT OF MENU INPUT CHOICE

CHOICE	NO DATA PRESENT	DATA PRESENT
OLD DATA	NEW DATA SUB-MENU	DATA MODIFICATION OR ADDITION ALLOWED
NEW DATA	NEW DATA SUB-MENU	NEW DATA SCREEN OPTIONS

The effects of these choices are explained in detail in the next sections.

NEW DATA SUB-MENU is a menu with the following choices:

   START NEW - allows you to manually input financial statements. This choice is almost identical to the OLD DATA option except that it precedes the entry of financial data by prompting for the Company Name, the scale (e.g., $millions or $000) and the earliest year of data to be input.

   IMPORT - allows you to recall a previously SAVED set of financial statements. See pages 86 - 90 for more information on SAVE and IMPORT

   LAST MENU - returns you to the TEMPLATE MENU shown above. This option allows you to "change your mind" or "escape" from the NEW DATA SUB-MENU.

DATA MODIFICATION OR ADDITION ALLOWED: presents a sub-menu that allows you to modify existing data. The menu options are as follows:

   NUMBERS - allows you to move around the Income Statement and Balance Sheet entering or modifying data in the input cells. (The input cells are all cells in the financial statements that are not totals or subtotals.)

   HEADER - enables you to change the Company Name, the scale (if any) directly under the Company Name and the beginning year (the year over the left-most data column).

Generally the NUMBERS choice is the one that will be chosen. It should also be noted that the NUMBERS choice should be used if there is a need to view the financial statements.

NEW DATA SCREEN OPTIONS: If data has been entered into the template and not saved, the NEW DATA option will send you to an option screen to find out what you want done with the existing data. The options are as follows:

   SAVE DATA to Disk before Erasing it from Screen

   ERASE IT without Saving Data to Disk

   RETURN TO CONTINUE PROCESSING THE EXISTING DATA allows you to "change your mind" or "escape." This choice allows you to continue working with the data on the screen without saving it.

EXPLANATION OF CERTAIN INPUTS

The input items are those accounts which make up the Income Statement and Balance Sheet. The format provided for these statements in the template is rather general. There may be occasions when the data you are to enter have different account names or more or less accounts than provided. There is no provision in the model that allows for account name changes. It is permissible to leave some accounts blank.

CALCULATING THE RESULTS

While entering data, press <RET> without entering a number. Calculation will be performed automatically by the program. The program will return to the TEMPLATE MENU after calculation is complete. IMPORTANT: Do not use the LOTUS <F9> key to calculate.

CHECKSUM

It is important that financial statement data be input correctly. An aid to ascertaining whether the Balance Sheet has been entered correctly is provided via the CHECKSUM row. This row, at the bottom of the Balance Sheet, is Total Assets minus Total Liabilities. If the Balance Sheet "balances," this row will be filled with zeros. Anything else indicates an "imbalance" and an error somewhere in the Balance Sheet input.

> **To use this aid, you must first CALCULATE the template, and then use the OLD DATA option to view the line.**

While there is not a corresponding line to ensure correctness for the Income Statement, its correctness can be checked rather easily. After the template has been calculated, make sure that the Net Profit amounts agree exactly with the source data. If they do, then you have input the information correctly.

It should be noted that both checking methods above are near, but not absolutely perfect, guarantees for correctness. It is possible to make two errors which perfectly offset one another. Because this event is so highly improbable, it is not something that users should be concerned with.

SAVE AND IMPORT COMMANDS
Data entered as financial statement information may be saved to the diskette (SAVE) and recalled (IMPORT) for processing or modification at a later date.

SAVE:
There are several opportunities for saving information. One may select the SAVE command from the TEMPLATE MENU at any time. This choice will allow you to save your data to disk and then to continue processing it. (It is a good practice to periodically use this option when entering lengthy financial information. It provides you with back-up information on disk in the event of a power failure or other mishap.) The other opportunities to save data occur whenever there is unsaved data in the template and an attempt is made to bring in new data (NEW DATA) or leave the template (END). In both cases you will be asked whether you wish to save the data with the screen shown as Exhibit XVII-1.

EXHIBIT XVII-1

(SCREEN FACSIMILE)

IMPORTANT: FINANCIAL DATA ALREADY IN FILE. DO YOU WANT TO:

===

1   SAVE DATA to Disk before Erasing it from Screen

2   ERASE IT without Saving Data to Disk

3   RETURN TO CONTINUE PROCESSING THE EXISTING DATA

ENTER NUMBER OF YOUR CHOICE:

Choose either 1, 2 or 3 and press <RET>. Note that numbers 1 and 2 both clear the financial statements. Selection 1, however, allows you to save the data to a diskette file prior to disposing of the screen data. Item 3 returns you to the TEMPLATE MENU, neither saving data nor altering the data on the screen. The following sections provide more information on saving data.

HOW TO SAVE DATA:

When a SAVE is requested, you will get the following screen:

```
       S A V I N G   F I N A N C I A L   S T A T E M E N T S
~~~~~~~~~~~~~~~~~~~~~~~~~~~~~~~~~~~~~~~~~~~~~~~~~~~~~~~~~~~~~~~~~~
          Choice                      Action
       ++++++++++++++++++++++++++++++++++++++++++++++++++++++++++++
       +                                                          +
       +    1              SAVE TO "WORKFILE"                     +
       +                                                          +
       +    2              SAVE TO COMPANY FILENAME               +
       +                                                          +
       +    3              DO NOT SAVE; RETURN TO TEMPLATE MENU   +
       ++++++++++++++++++++++++++++++++++++++++++++++++++++++++++++
    CAUTION!!!      CAUTION!!!  CAUTION!!!     CAUTION!!!    CAUTION!!!
    **************************************************************
       CHOOSE FILE NAME CAREFULLY!!!! IF A FILE ALREADY EXISTS, IT
           WILL BE OVERWRITTEN WITH THESE FINANCIAL STATEMENTS.
    **************************************************************
    CAUTION!!!      CAUTION!!!  CAUTION!!!     CAUTION!!!    CAUTION!!!
                        SELECT YOUR CHOICE
------------------------------------------------------------------
```

A selection is made by entering a number from 1 to 3 and pressing <RET>. An explanation of the three choices follows:

SAVE TO "WORKFILE" (1) - automatically saves financial statements to a file on disk named WORKFILE. Any data that was previously in this file will be overwritten by the data currently on screen.

SAVE TO COMPANY FILENAME (2) - choosing this option causes a partial filename starting with "X" to appear on the screen. (See THE "HELPFUL HINT - NAMING FINANCIAL DATA" on the next page for the rationale for beginning Company names with an "X.") Add up to seven more letters to the "X" for a filename. Although most characters are permissible, check the LOTUS or MS DOS manuals if you intend to use a name with an unusual keyboard character. (Should you wish to use a different naming convention than the "X" approach, you may erase the "X" by using the backspace on your keyboard and then type up to eight new letters for the filename.) After typing the filename, press <RET> to save the data to a file with that name. If a file already exists with that name, its contents will be automatically overwritten with the data currently on screen.

DO NOT SAVE; RETURN TO TEMPLATE MENU (3) - this choice returns the user to the TEMPLATE MENU. No data is altered or saved. The user merely returns to processing whatever data is on the screen.

When saving data, remember the following two points:

1. CHOICES 1 AND 2 MAY CAUSE DATA SAVED ON DISK TO BE OVER-WRITTEN. If there is an existing file on your disk with the same name, IT WILL BE OVERWRITTEN, AND THE OLD CONTENTS OF THAT FILE WILL BE LOST!!

2. NEVER USE ANY NAME IDENTICAL TO THE TEMPLATE NAMES, OR THE TEMPLATES WILL BE OVERWRITTEN.

HELPFUL HINT: WORKFILE VERSUS COMPANY NAME
Should you save your data to WORKFILE or to a COMPANY NAME? While this choice is as much personal preference as anything else, this author favors using the workfile when working with data. When data is finally fully entered into the FINSTATE model, this author saves it to the workfile and then to a company name (see next hint for naming companies) on diskette.

(REMEMBER: SAVE YOUR DATA FREQUENTLY. DO NOT TRY TO INPUT IT ALL AND THEN SAVE IT. Frequent saves are made to the workfile. Only the final save is made to a company-named file.)

At this point, the company data is on diskette in two files: the workfile and the company-named file. This author prefers this approach because he feels that it reduces the chances of writing over a valuable file. Subsequent analysis with the other models in this section is performed on the workfile.

HELPFUL HINT: NAMING FINANCIAL DATA
If you are going to be saving financial data from many different companies to diskette, it is sometimes helpful to "tag" like files in some way. An example might be to start all saved financial data files with the same infrequent character. As an example, precede all saved financial data file names with the letter X. So, when you look at your files and see XHAPPY, XIBM, XGENMTRS, XALCOA, etc. they will all stand out and easily be recognizable as files that contain financial data that can be used with FINSTATE or the other models in this section.

Chapter 17: Financial Statements

WHAT IS SAVED:
The Income Statement and the Balance Sheet are saved.

HELPFUL HINT: BACKING UP FINSTATE-CREATED FILES
For the same reasons that it was important to back-up the original CMF diskettes, it is important to back-up the financial files that a user creates. Having a financial file saved to XHAPPY and WORKFILE is not a satisfactory back-up for two reasons:

1. WORKFILE is a file designed to be used over and over. When you use it again, the previously saved data is overwritten.

2. Both files reside on the same disk which does not protect against losing or damaging the disk. This comment applies to both hard and floppy disks.

A user should save financial files to the hard disk and also to a separate floppy diskette. There are two ways to save financial files to a back-up diskette:

1. From FINSTATE: When the file is completed and saved to a hard disk, place your back-up CMF floppy diskette into drive A. Select the SAVE option from the FINSTATE menu. Select OTHER and for the company name type **A:<company name><RET>**. For company name you would insert the company name, e.g. XHAPPY. The file will now be saved to the CMF back-up diskette in drive A. (NOTE: if you work with many companies, you may run out of space on the CMF back-up diskette. You may use any floppy diskette to back-up company files.)

2. From DOS: At the **C:\CMF** prompt with a floppy diskette in drive A, type the following:

   copy filename.* A:<RET>

Do not actually type "filename" but type the name of the file which you wish to back-up. For example, **XHAPPY.WKS** in the case of the file provided on your diskette. If you have used "X" as in XHAPPY to precede all company files, you may use the command:

   copy X*.* A:<RET>

This command will copy all files beginning with X to drive A.

IMPORT:
Data that has been saved to disk may be called back into the Financial Statements template via the IMPORT command. The command will prompt you for a file name. Type the name of the file and press <RET>. The financial statements will appear on the screen, and all the ratios will be automatically calculated. One file has been included on your disk for use with the IMPORT command. This file is named XHAPPY and will be used in the problem at the end of this chapter.

CAUTION: IMPORTING ANY FILE OTHER THAN A COMPANY DATA FILE WILL RENDER THE FINSTATE TEMPLATE UNUSABLE.

If you accidentally retrieve a non-data file, do not try to use the template. Reload the FINSTATE template and start over.

HELPFUL HINT: USING THE IMPORT COMMAND TO CHANGE WORKFILES
For users who will be doing substantial financial statement analysis and who wish to use the workfile rather than company-named files (as in the author's helpful hint above) in the analysis, the FINSTATE model and the IMPORT command provide the means of shifting different companies financial data into the WORKFILE. Suppose, for example you have three company files on diskette: Comp1, Comp2 and Comp3. Suppose you want to perform a ratio analysis and a common size analysis on Comp3. The following steps will enable you to accomplish your objective:

1. Load FINSTATE.
2. Select IMPORT and import Comp3.
3. Select SAVE and save to WORKFILE. (Note that Comp3 data is still on diskette under file Comp3 and also now in the WORKFILE.)
4. Quit FINSTATE and load up either RATIO or COMSIZE.
5. Select DATA option and then WORKFILE option.
6. The Comp3 data will appear and be analyzed automatically.

TECHNICAL INFORMATION AND TEMPLATE LIMITATIONS
The template is limited to a maximum of five years of financial data.

COMPANY ON DISK
One company is provided on disk under the file name XHAPPY. This same data is also included in the WORKFILE. You may IMPORT either of these files to duplicate the results shown in the sample problem included below.

PROBLEM
Input the financial statements of the Happy Daze Company (shown below) and save them to diskette. (DO NOT TYPE IN EACH NUMBER BELOW. See SOLUTION before proceeding.)

SOLUTION

Choose OLD DATA or NEW DATA option. If you choose START NEW at the next menu prompt, you may input all of the data manually. If you choose IMPORT and then select WORKFILE, the data will automatically appear on the screen. You may also choose IMPORT and then select OTHER and, when prompted, type **XHAPPY**<RET> and the same data will be brought to the screen.

INCOME STATEMENT
HAPPY DAZE
($000)

FOR YEARS:	1989	1990	1991	1992	1993
REVENUES	$33,000	$35,893	$42,555	$52,108	$62,319
Cost of Sales	$22,841	$24,407	$29,972	$38,412	$47,719
GROSS MARGIN	$10,159	$11,486	$12,583	$13,696	$14,600
Selling	$3,214	$3,975	$4,113	$4,675	$4,896
Administrative	$2,500	$2,734	$3,041	$3,455	$3,815
Other	$640	$530	$785	$905	$1,054
TOTAL SG&A	$6,354	$7,239	$7,939	$9,035	$9,765
OPERATING INC.	$3,805	$4,247	$4,644	$4,661	$4,835
Other Inc/(Exp)					
Interest Exp.	$482	$505	$453	$466	$691
PRE-TAX INCOME	$3,323	$3,742	$4,191	$4,195	$4,144
Income Taxes	$1,174	$1,281	$1,412	$1,300	$1,311
NET PROFIT	$2,149	$2,461	$2,779	$2,895	$2,833
EPS	$1.07	$1.23	$1.39	$1.45	$1.42
Div/Share	$0.10	$0.15	$0.20	$0.20	$0.20

BALANCE SHEET

HAPPY DAZE
($000)

FOR YEARS:	1989	1990	1991	1992	1993
CURRENT ASSETS:					
Cash	$422	$1,481	$1,281	$1,247	$1,532
Accts. Rec.	$3,626	$3,702	$4,783	$6,377	$7,476
Inventories	$5,162	$4,460	$4,872	$5,983	$6,913
Other Current	$725	$877	$910	$988	$1,031
TOTAL CURRENT	$9,935	$10,520	$11,846	$14,595	$16,952
PROPERTY:					
Plant & Equip.	$5,995	$6,100	$7,900	$10,100	$13,421
Accum. Deprec.					
Net Plant	$5,995	$6,100	$7,900	$10,100	$13,421
Other					
NET PROPERTY	$5,995	$6,100	$7,900	$10,100	$13,421
OTHER ASSETS	$1,550	$2,070	$1,934	$1,934	$2,134
TOTAL	$17,480	$18,690	$21,680	$26,629	$32,507
CURR. LIAB.:					
Accounts Pay.	$3,654	$2,890	$3,187	$4,671	$6,200
Accr. Liab.	$1,020	$842	$1,234	$1,538	$1,844
Notes Payable	$560	$640	$0	$600	$600
S.T. Debt	$880	$1,031	$1,500	$378	$212
TOTAL CURRENT	$6,114	$5,403	$5,921	$7,187	$8,856
LONG-TERM DEBT					
Notes Payable	$640	$0	$0	$1,200	$600
Bonds	$2,000	$2,500	$2,500	$2,500	$4,000
Bank Debt	$0	$0	$0	$0	$800
TOTAL L.T. DEBT	$2,640	$2,500	$2,500	$3,700	$5,400
OTHER LIAB.:					
Def. Inc. Tax	$250	$150	$243	$231	$307
TOTAL OTHER	$250	$150	$243	$231	$307
EQUITY:					
Common Stock	$1,200	$1,200	$1,200	$1,200	$1,200
Capital Surplus	$2,150	$2,150	$2,150	$2,150	$2,150
Ret. Earnings	$5,126	$7,287	$9,666	$12,161	$14,594
TOTAL EQUITY	$8,476	$10,637	$13,016	$15,511	$17,944
TOTAL	$17,480	$18,690	$21,680	$26,629	$32,507

Chapter 18 RATIO ANALYSIS

PURPOSE: To calculate financial ratios

LOADING THE TEMPLATE
From the STATEMENT ANALYSIS sub-menu choose number: 2
From LOTUS choose file name: RATIO

TEMPLATE MENU: Menu choices available are as follows:
   DATA - to import financial statements from diskette
   VIEW - view financial ratios
   GRAPH - view output in graph form
   PRINT - prints income statement, balance sheet and financial
           ratios
   HELP - allows user to view help screen
   END - allows the user to leave this template

HOW TO INPUT DATA: Choose DATA menu option. The user cannot use the keyboard to enter or modify data. Financial Statement data must be imported from file on disk. Choosing the DATA option will produce a sub-menu where the user will be asked to choose either WORKFILE or OTHER. These choices provide the following results:

   WORKFILE - imports the financial statements previously saved
   to "workfile"

   OTHER - prompts the user for a file name from which financial
   statements will be imported

CAUTION REGARDING INP: If the user chooses OTHER, it is important that a proper file be imported. If a file is imported that does not contain financial data created and saved via the FINSTATE model, the results are unpredictable. The user should immediately terminate the program by either re-booting the PC or choosing the END option from the menu.

CALCULATING THE RESULTS
Calculations are done automatically when financial data is imported. IMPORTANT: Do not use the LOTUS <F9> key to calculate.

TECHNICAL INFORMATION AND TEMPLATE LIMITATIONS
The template is limited to five years of data.
Turnover ratios are calculated using the asset balance for the particular year rather than averaging beginning and ending balances.

PROBLEM:
Calculate financial ratios for the Happy Daze Company.

SOLUTION:
Choose DATA. Select WORKFILE (assuming that Happy Daze financial statements are still in the workfile) or select OTHER and type **XHAPPY**<RET> when prompted for the file name. Choose the VIEW or PRINT option to see Exhibit XVIII-1 below:

EXHIBIT XVIII-1

HAPPY DAZE
FINANCIAL RATIOS

FOR YEARS:	1989	1990	1991	1992	1993	AVERAGE
TURNOVER RATIOS:						
Total Assets	1.89	1.92	1.96	1.96	1.92	1.93
Fixed Assets	5.50	5.88	5.39	5.16	4.64	5.32
Current Assets	3.32	3.41	3.59	3.57	3.68	3.51
Receivables	9.10	9.70	8.90	8.17	8.34	8.84
Inventory	4.42	5.47	6.15	6.42	6.90	5.87
Payables	6.25	8.45	9.40	8.22	7.70	8.00
TURNOVER - DAYS:						
Total Assets	193.3	190.1	186.0	186.5	190.4	189.3
Fixed Assets	66.3	62.0	67.8	70.7	78.6	69.1
Current Assets	109.9	107.0	101.6	102.2	99.3	104.0
Receivables	40.1	37.6	41.0	44.7	43.8	41.4
Inventory	82.5	66.7	59.3	56.9	52.9	63.6
Payables	58.4	43.2	38.8	44.4	47.4	46.4
LEVERAGE:						
Liab./Assets	51.51%	43.09%	39.96%	41.75%	44.80%	44.22%
Liab./Equity	106.23%	75.71%	66.56%	71.68%	81.16%	80.27%
LT Debt/Equity	31.15%	23.50%	19.21%	23.85%	30.09%	25.56%
LIQUIDITY:						
Working Capital	$3,821	$5,117	$5,925	$7,408	$8,096	$6,073
Current Ratio	1.62	1.95	2.00	2.03	1.91	1.90
Quick Ratio	0.78	1.12	1.18	1.20	1.13	1.08
COVERAGE:						
Interest	7.89	8.41	10.25	10.00	7.00	8.71

(Exhibit continued on next page)

EXHIBIT XVIII-1 (Continued)

HAPPY DAZE
FINANCIAL RATIOS

FOR YEARS:	1989	1990	1991	1982	1993	AVERAGE
PROFITABILITY:						
Gross Margin	30.78%	32.00%	29.57%	26.28%	23.43%	28.41%
Operating Inc.	11.53%	11.83%	10.91%	8.94%	7.76%	10.20%
Income B.Tax	10.07%	10.43%	9.85%	8.05%	6.65%	9.01%
Net Profit	6.51%	6.86%	6.53%	5.56%	4.55%	6.00%
OI/Assets	21.77%	22.72%	21.42%	17.50%	14.87%	19.66%
Profit/Assets	12.29%	13.17%	12.82%	10.87%	8.72%	11.57%
Profit/Equity	25.35%	23.14%	21.35%	18.66%	15.79%	20.86%
DUPONT ANALYSIS:						
ASSET TURNOVER	1.89	1.92	1.96	1.96	1.92	1.93
times ROS	6.51%	6.86%	6.53%	5.56%	4.55%	6.00%
= ROI (ROA)	12.29%	13.17%	12.82%	10.87%	8.72%	11.57%
times LEVERAGE	2.06	1.76	1.67	1.72	1.81	1.80
= ROE	25.35%	23.14%	21.35%	18.66%	15.79%	20.86%

Chapter 19 COMMON SIZE ANALYSIS

PURPOSE: To calculate common size (index) analysis

LOADING THE TEMPLATE
From the STATEMENT ANALYSIS sub-menu choose number: 3
From LOTUS choose file name: COMSIZE

TEMPLATE MENU: Menu choices available are as follows:
   DATA - to import financial statements
   VIEW - view financial ratios
   GRAPH - view output in graph form
   PRINT - prints income statement, balance sheet and financial
         ratios
   HELP - allows user to view help screen
   END - allows the user to leave this template

HOW TO INPUT DATA: Choose DATA menu option. The user cannot use the keyboard to enter or modify data. Financial Statement data must be imported from file on disk. Choosing the DATA option will produce a sub-menu where the user will be asked to choose either WORKFILE or OTHER. These choices provide the following results:

   WORKFILE - imports the financial statements previously saved to "workfile"

   OTHER - prompts the user for a file name from which financial statements will be imported

CAUTION REGARDING INP: If the user chooses OTHER, it is important that a proper file be imported. If a file is imported that does not contain financial data <u>created and saved via the FINSTATE model</u>, the results are unpredictable. The user should immediately terminate the program by either re-booting the PC or choosing the END option from the menu.

CALCULATING THE RESULTS
Calculations are done automatically when financial data is imported. IMPORTANT: Do not use the LOTUS <F9> key to calculate.

TECHNICAL INFORMATION AND TEMPLATE LIMITATIONS
The template is limited to five years of data.
All data, including balance sheet accounts, are shown as a percentage of sales

PROBLEM:
Prepare a Common Size statement for the Happy Daze Company.

SOLUTION:
Choose DATA. Select WORKFILE (assuming that Happy Daze financial statements are still in the workfile) or select OTHER and type XHAPPY <RET> when prompted for the file name. Choose the VIEW or PRINT option to see the following income statement and balance sheet expressed as a percentage of sales:

```
COMMON SIZE ANALYSIS -- INCOME STATEMENT
                              HAPPY DAZE
                      P E R C E N T A G E   O F   S A L E S
       FOR YEARS:      1989      1990      1991      1992      1993
       ~~~~~~~~~~~~~~~~~~~~~~~~~~~~~~~~~~~~~~~~~~~~~~~~~~~~~~~~~~~~
       REVENUES      100.00%   100.00%   100.00%   100.00%   100.00%
       Cost of Sales  69.22%    68.00%    70.43%    73.72%    76.57%
       ------------------------------------------------------------
       GROSS MARGIN   30.78%    32.00%    29.57%    26.28%    23.43%
       ------------------------------------------------------------
       Depreciation    0.00%     0.00%     0.00%     0.00%     0.00%
       Selling         9.74%    11.07%     9.67%     8.97%     7.86%
       Administrative  7.58%     7.62%     7.15%     6.63%     6.12%
       Other           1.94%     1.48%     1.84%     1.74%     1.69%
       ------------------------------------------------------------
       TOTAL SG&A     19.25%    20.17%    18.66%    17.34%    15.67%
       ------------------------------------------------------------
       OPERATING INC. 11.53%    11.83%    10.91%     8.94%     7.76%
       Other Inc/(Exp) 0.00%     0.00%     0.00%     0.00%     0.00%
       Interest Exp.   1.46%     1.41%     1.06%     0.89%     1.11%
       ------------------------------------------------------------
       PRE-TAX INCOME 10.07%    10.43%     9.85%     8.05%     6.65%
       Income Taxes    3.56%     3.57%     3.32%     2.49%     2.10%
       ------------------------------------------------------------
       NET PROFIT      6.51%     6.86%     6.53%     5.56%     4.55%
       ============================================================
```

COMMON SIZE ANALYSIS - BALANCE SHEET
HAPPY DAZE
PERCENTAGE OF SALES

	1989	1990	1991	1992	1993
CURRENT ASSETS					
Cash	1.28%	4.13%	3.01%	2.39%	2.46%
Mkt. Securities	0.00%	0.00%	0.00%	0.00%	0.00%
Accts. Rec.	10.99%	10.31%	11.24%	12.24%	12.00%
Inventories	15.64%	12.43%	11.45%	11.48%	11.09%
Other Current	2.20%	2.44%	2.14%	1.90%	1.65%
TOTAL CURRENT	30.11%	29.31%	27.84%	28.01%	27.20%
PROPERTY:					
Plant & Equip.	18.17%	16.99%	18.56%	19.38%	21.54%
Accum. Deprec.	0.00%	0.00%	0.00%	0.00%	0.00%
Net Plant	18.17%	16.99%	18.56%	19.38%	21.54%
Other	0.00%	0.00%	0.00%	0.00%	0.00%
NET PROPERTY	18.17%	16.99%	18.56%	19.38%	21.54%
OTHER ASSETS	4.70%	5.77%	4.54%	3.71%	3.42%
TOTAL ASSETS	52.97%	52.07%	50.95%	51.10%	52.16%

	1989	1990	1991	1992	1993
CURR. LIAB.:					
Accounts Pay.	11.07%	8.05%	7.49%	8.96%	9.95%
Accr. Liab.	3.09%	2.35%	2.90%	2.95%	2.96%
Notes Payable	1.70%	1.78%	0.00%	1.15%	0.96%
S.T. Debt	2.67%	2.87%	3.52%	0.73%	0.34%
TOTAL CURRENT	18.53%	15.05%	13.91%	13.79%	14.21%
LONG-TERM DEBT					
Notes Payable	1.94%	0.00%	0.00%	2.30%	0.96%
Bonds	6.06%	6.97%	5.87%	4.80%	6.42%
Bank Debt	0.00%	0.00%	0.00%	0.00%	1.28%
TOTAL L.T. DEBT	8.00%	6.97%	5.87%	7.10%	8.67%
OTHER LIABILITIES:					
Non-curr. Accr.	0.00%	0.00%	0.00%	0.00%	0.00%
Def. Inc. Tax	0.76%	0.42%	0.57%	0.44%	0.49%
TOTAL OTHER	0.76%	0.42%	0.57%	0.44%	0.49%
EQUITY					
Common Stock	3.64%	3.34%	2.82%	2.30%	1.93%
Capital Surplus	6.52%	5.99%	5.05%	4.13%	3.45%
Ret. Earnings	15.53%	20.30%	22.71%	23.34%	23.42%
TOTAL EQUITY	25.68%	29.64%	30.59%	29.77%	28.79%
TOTAL	52.97%	52.07%	50.95%	51.10%	52.16%

Chapter 20 CHANGES IN FINANCIAL POSITION

PURPOSE: To calculate changes in financial position by year and cumulatively for up to five years of financial data.

LOADING THE TEMPLATE
From the STATEMENT ANALYSIS sub-menu choose number: 4
From LOTUS choose file name: FUNDSFLO

TEMPLATE MENU: Menu choices available are as follows:
   DATA - to import financial statements
   VIEW - view financial ratios
   PRINT - prints income statement, balance sheet and financial
           ratios
   HELP - allows user to view help screen
   END - allows the user to leave this template

HOW TO INPUT DATA: Choose DATA menu option. The user cannot use the keyboard to enter or modify data. Financial Statement data must be imported from file on disk. Choosing the DATA option will produce a sub-menu where the user will be asked to choose either WORKFILE or OTHER. These choices provide the following results:

   WORKFILE - imports the financial statements previously saved
   to "workfile"

   OTHER - prompts the user for a file name from which financial
   statements will be imported

CAUTION REGARDING INP: If the user chooses OTHER, it is important that a proper file be imported. If a file is imported that does not contain financial data <u>created and saved via the FINSTATE model</u>, the results are unpredictable. The user should immediately terminate the program by either re-booting the PC or choosing the END option from the menu.

CALCULATING THE RESULTS
Calculations are done automatically when financial data is imported. IMPORTANT: Do not use the LOTUS <F9> key to calculate.

TECHNICAL INFORMATION AND TEMPLATE LIMITATIONS
The template can only handle five years of financial data.

PROBLEM:
Prepare a Statement of Changes in Financial Position for the Happy Daze Company. Show the cumulative changes for the five year period.

SOLUTION:
Choose DATA. Select WORKFILE (assuming that Happy Daze financial statements are still in the workfile) or select OTHER and type XHAPPY <RET> when prompted for the file name. Choose the VIEW or PRINT option to see the data shown as Exhibit XX-1 on the next page.

EXHIBIT XX-1

STATEMENT OF CHANGES IN FINANCIAL POSITION
HAPPY DAZE
($000)

	1990	1991	1992	1993	TOTAL
Cash	$1,059	($200)	($34)	$285	$1,110
Accts. Rec.	$76	$1,081	$1,594	$1,099	$3,850
Inventories	($702)	$412	$1,111	$930	$1,751
Other Current	$152	$33	$78	$43	$306
TOTAL CURRENT	$585	$1,326	$2,749	$2,357	$7,017
PROPERTY:					
Net Plant	$105	$1,800	$2,200	$3,321	$7,426
NET PROPERTY	$105	$1,800	$2,200	$3,321	$7,426
OTHER ASSETS	$520	($136)	$0	$200	$584
TOTAL	$1,210	$2,990	$4,949	$5,878	$15,027
CURR. LIAB.:					
Accounts Pay.	($764)	$297	$1,484	$1,529	$2,546
Accr. Liab.	($178)	$392	$304	$306	$824
Notes Payable	$80	($640)	$600	$0	$40
S.T. Debt	$151	$469	($1,122)	($166)	($668)
TOTAL CURRENT	($711)	$518	$1,266	$1,669	$2,742
LONG-TERM DEBT					
Notes Payable	($640)	$0	$1,200	($600)	($40)
Bonds	$500	$0	$0	$1,500	$2,000
Bank Debt	$0	$0	$0	$800	$800
TOTAL L.T. DEBT	($140)	$0	$1,200	$1,700	$2,760
OTHER LIAB.:					
Def. Inc. Tax	($100)	$93	($12)	$76	$57
TOTAL OTHER	($100)	$93	($12)	$76	$57
EQUITY:					
Common Stock	$0	$0	$0	$0	$0
Capital Surplus	$0	$0	$0	$0	$0
Ret. Earnings	$2,161	$2,379	$2,495	$2,433	$9,468
TOTAL EQUITY	$2,161	$2,379	$2,495	$2,433	$9,468
TOTAL	$1,210	$2,990	$4,949	$5,878	$15,027
CHG W'KNG CAP.	$1,296	$808	$1,483	$688	$4,275

Chapter 21 PRO FORMA STATEMENTS

PURPOSE: To project financial statements for a three-year period. An automatic forecast will be produced. The automatic forecast is user-modifiable.

MODEL COMPLEXITY
The interaction problem (discussed below) creates certain mechanical problems that can be overcome only via some complex programming techniques (e.g. use of the CIRC programming technique discussed below). The user does not have to solve these programming complexities, but these complexities do reflect themselves in the somewhat more detailed documentation required to correctly use this model.

A user should understand this documentation before trying to use this model.

<u>CAUTION</u>   <u>CAUTION</u>   <u>CAUTION</u>   <u>CAUTION</u>   <u>CAUTION</u>

Make sure that the use of ASSUMPTIONS and OVERRIDE for modifying data is fully understood before trying to use them.
<u>CAUTION</u>   <u>CAUTION</u>   <u>CAUTION</u>   <u>CAUTION</u>   <u>CAUTION</u>

LOADING THE TEMPLATE
From the STATEMENT ANALYSIS sub-menu choose number: 5
From LOTUS choose file name: PLAN

TEMPLATE MENU
Menu choices available are as follows:

    DATA - to import financial statements
    ASSUMPTIONS - to view or change the assumptions
    OVERRIDE - to view or override the pro forma statements
    PRINT - prints the pro forma financial statements
    CALC - calculates the spreadsheet three times
    HELP - view help screen
    END - leave this template

VIEW is not available as a menu option. To view the data in the pro forma financial statements, choose OVERRIDE and merely move around the spreadsheet without entering a number. Choose ASSUMPTIONS to view the assumptions which were used to create the pro forma statements, and move around without entering a number.

HOW TO INPUT DATA: Choose DATA menu option. The user cannot use the keyboard to enter or modify data using the DATA option (see ASSUMPTIONS and OVERRIDE options which enable the forecast to be modified). Financial Statement data must be imported from file on disk. Choosing the DATA option will produce a sub-menu where the user will be asked to choose either WORKFILE or OTHER. These choices provide the following results:

>   WORKFILE - imports the financial statements previously saved to "workfile"

>   OTHER - prompts the user for a file name from which financial statements will be imported

CAUTION REGARDING INP: If the user chooses OTHER, it is important that a proper file be imported. If a file is imported that does not contain financial data <u>created and saved via the FINSTATE model</u>, the results are unpredictable. The user should immediately terminate the program by either re-booting the PC or choosing the END option from the menu.

THE INTERACTION PROBLEM AND CONVERGENCE
Forecasting financial statements, whether done manually or via a computer, involves a calculation difficulty because of an interaction between the income statement and the balance sheet. This interaction problem involves the relationships between debt, interest and profit. Specifically:

>   Profit depends on Interest Expense
>   Retained Earnings depends on Profit
>   Debt depends on Retained Earnings
>   Interest Expense depends on Debt

This relationship is circular in the sense that a change in any one produces changes in the others, which produce an additional change in the first, which produces changes in the others, which .... etc. etc.. Each change in a particular variable should become progressively smaller until it finally converges on a number that will not change. To reach such convergence, however, may require a number of iterations.

CIRC REFERENCE
Programming a circular relationship in a spreadsheet produces what, in spreadsheet terminology, is known as a circular reference. (This is the reason you see the CIRC warning on your screen.) It is circular because the answer to one variable is dependent upon the answer to another variable, which itself is dependent upon the answer to the first variable. While the CIRC reference usually signals that you have made an error in your spreadsheet programming, in this particular model it is a deliberate and necessary element in order to deal with the interaction problem.

"PLUG" ACCOUNTS

A balance must be achieved in the pro forma Balance Sheet. The process of forecasting involves "plugging" an account or accounts to achieve this balance. Two accounts are used as "plug" accounts in the PLAN model. These accounts are Marketable Securities and Notes Payable (current liability). If there is a shortage of cash, the Notes Payable account will be used to "borrow" the cash shortfall. An excess of cash is reflected in the Marketable Securities account. Only one of these accounts will be used in any particular forecast year. For example, if there is a cash shortage, Notes Payable will be used and Marketable Securities will show as zero.

CALCULATING THE RESULTS

IMPORTANT: Do not use the LOTUS <F9> key to calculate. Use the CALC menu option (discussed below) to perform calculations.

ACCEPTING THE AUTOMATIC FORECAST

This model produces an automatic forecast (3-year projected income statement and balance sheet). If a user agrees with the automatic forecast (i.e., no modifications are required), then the user must ensure that the automatic forecast has converged.

The CALC option must be used to achieve convergence

It should be pointed out that the automatic forecast cannot forecast the number of shares outstanding because this data is not a part of the FINSTATE financial statements. This information is not necessary unless dividends are to be paid in the forecast period (or unless the user wishes to have EPS calculated in the forecast period).

If dividends (either preferred or common) are to be paid, the user must modify the forecast (see MODIFYING THE AUTOMATIC FORECAST and the ASSUMPTIONS sections below).

CALC MENU OPTION

One calculation is done automatically when financial data is imported. Because of the interaction problem (discussed above), **multiple calculations are required**. A detailed discussion of the CALC option follows on the next page.

WHAT HAPPENS WHEN THE CALC OPTION IS SELECTED?
The CALC menu option allows the user to calculate (re-calculate) the spreadsheet. Each time the CALC menu option is chosen, the spreadsheet will be calculated (re-calculated) three times. Because the spreadsheet is rather large, it takes a bit of time to do a calculation. The amount of time required will depend upon the computer that you are using and how fast it processes information. While the calculations are taking place, the WAIT signal that Lotus 1-2-3 uses will be blinking (at the top right-hand portion of the spreadsheet). When calculations have stopped, the WAIT signal will disappear, and you will see the TEMPLATE MENU reappear.

HOW MANY TIMES SHOULD THE CALC OPTION BE SELECTED?
There is no simple rule to determine how many re-calculations will be required to solve the interaction problem. Generally two selections of the CALC menu option (six re-calculations) should be sufficient. If convergence has not been achieved after 4 CALC choices (12 re-calculations), it probably cannot be achieved. The user should inspect the assumptions to determine what assumption is causing the problem.

HOW DOES ONE DETERMINE WHETHER CONVERGENCE HAS BEEN ACHIEVED?
When the CALC option is chosen, the user is moved to a portion of the pro forma statements where he can see the Interest Expense and Pre-tax Profit line. As the model re-calculates, the user will see successive changes in both of these accounts. Each subsequent change should be smaller than the prior one.

> At some point, a re-calculation produces no change in the Interest Expense (or Profit) figure which signifies convergence.

It is important to note, however, that:

> After convergence has been achieved, additional modification of any data via either the ASSUMPTIONS or OVERRIDE options will necessitate the repetition of CALC until a new convergence is achieved.

MODIFYING THE AUTOMATIC FORECAST
While the automatic forecast generated by the model may sometimes be satisfactory, the judgment exercised by the model is rather mechanical and generally not as satisfactory as an informed user's judgment. For this reason, provision is made for the user to override or customize the forecast to fit his best estimates of the future. The two menu options which provide this flexibility are the ASSUMPTIONS and OVERRIDE options.

For the user who is to modify the automatic forecasts produced by
the model (and this will be 95% or more of users), it is necessary for a user to fully understand how to use the ASSUMPTIONS
and OVERRIDE menu options so as to avoid making mistakes that
will result in poor or erroneous forecasts.

**Do not attempt to modify a forecast without fully reading
and understanding the sections below on ASSUMPTIONS, OVER-
RIDE and A SUMMARY OUTLINE FOR USING THIS MODEL.**

ASSUMPTIONS

ASSUMPTIONS allows a user to modify a collection of assumptions.
Selection of this menu option moves the user to an historical
summary of key statistics. No input can be made in this first
screen (see SOLUTION below for a representation of this screen).
Using the cursor keys, move down to the assumptions screen (press
the END key [number 1 on keypad] to move immediately to the
screen or use the cursor-down key multiple times to get there).
Shown as Exhibit XXI-1 is the assumptions screen.

EXHIBIT XXI-1

		1994	1995	1996
109	ASSUMPTIONS:			
110				
111	Revenue	$73,127	$85,809	$100,691
112	Rev. Inc -%	17.34%	17.34%	17.34%
113	GM - %	28.41%	28.41%	28.41%
114	SG&A	13321.8	15632.2	18343.3
115	SG&A - %	18.22%	18.22%	18.22%
116	Other Inc/(Exp)	0	0	0
117	Tax Rate -%	33.18%	33.18%	33.18%
118	Minimum Cash	1193	1193	1193
119	Other C.A. - %	25.84%	25.84%	25.84%
120	Net Plant	13842.1	16242.8	19059.8
121	Other Assets	3115.1	3655.4	4289.3
122	Non-debt CL-%	11.95%	11.95%	11.95%
123	Other Liabiliti	382.3	448.7	526.5
124	Int. Rate - %	10.00%	10.00%	10.00%
125	Div/Share	$0.20	$0.20	$0.20
126	Shares Outstand			
127	Tot'l Comm. Div	$0	$0	$0
128	Tot'l Pref. Div	$0.0	$0.0	$0.0

Certain cells are emboldened (brighter). It is these cells where your cursor may be moved and data may be entered. It should be noted that each of the emboldened cells contains a Lotus 1-2-3 formula that calculated the value in the cell from the actual (historical) financial statements with the exception of the following three items:

<u>Line 124 Int. Rate - %</u> This information cannot be obtained from the financial statements. This line has been arbitrarily set up at 10%. You may, of course, use any interest rates on this line that are applicable.

<u>Line 126 Shares Outstand</u> This information cannot be obtained from the financial statements. Line 26 is used to calculate Line 127, Tot'l Comm. Div, which is equal to Line 125 times Line 126. If the company will pay dividends during the forecast period you must reflect the amount in line 127. If you know the shares outstanding, it is recommended that you allow line 127 to calculate by inputting line 126 (and 125 if necessary). If this is not practical, you may overtype the total dividends on line 127. Either approach will feed the effects of the common dividend into the forecast after calculation. Whichever approach is used, make sure that the scale (e.g. $000 or whatever) is taken into account in your entries.

<u>Line 128 Tot'l Pref. Div</u> This information cannot be obtained from the financial statements. If paid, a user must type in the total for each year.

Typing over any cells which contain formulas (which are any of the cells shown in the assumptions block except those on Lines 124, 126 and 128) destroys the formulas and replaces the contents of the cell with the number entered. Regardless of how the numbers get into the assumptions block, they will be used to modify the pro forma statements (unless OVERRIDE has been used as discussed below). After calculation, the effects of your numbers may be seen in the forecasted data.

> **All ASSUMPTIONS changes should be made prior to using OVERRIDE. ASSUMPTIONS changes should not be made after making changes with OVERRIDE.**

It is, of course, permissible to make changes with ASSUMPTIONS, use OVERRIDE to <u>view</u> the changes, and then make more changes with ASSUMPTIONS.

Overwritten formulas are only destroyed on the screen. The file copy of the model has not been altered. When the model is reloaded from diskette, the formulas are restored. (NOTE: Importing new financial data re-sets the formulas to their original condition.)

OVERRIDE

OVERRIDE is a menu choice that should be used to do two things:

1. View the forecasted data.
2. Make final changes to the forecasted data.

OVERRIDE allows a user to view the pro forma statements. It also enables a user to modify those cells in the pro forma statements which show up as emboldened on the screen. Generally, these cells are those that are not totals or sub-totals.

OVERRIDE should be viewed as a "fine-tuning" option. That is, the major changes to a forecast should be made via the ASSUMPTIONS command.

OVERRIDE should be used after ASSUMPTIONS. Changes with ASSUMPTIONS should not be made after changes with OVERRIDE.

A SUMMARY OUTLINE FOR USING THIS MODEL

The following steps should be followed in using this model:

1. Load the model.
2. Import financial statements of a company.
3. Determine whether automatic forecast is acceptable.
    a. View Assumptions (use ASSUMPTIONS with no input).
    b. View Pro Forma Statements (use OVERRIDE with no input).
    c. If acceptable, go to number 7 below.
    d. If unacceptable, continue (go to 4 below).
4. Modify assumptions.
    a. Choose ASSUMPTIONS.
    b. Type over those assumptions you want to change.
    c. Press CALC key.
5. Review the Pro Forma Statements.
    a. Choose OVERRIDE.
    b. Review the numbers.
    c. If satisfactory, go to 7 below.
    d. If unsatisfactory, do one of the following:
        i. return to step 4 to modify more assumptions.
        ii. go to step 6.
6. "Fine-tune" the Forecast.
    a. Choose OVERRIDE.
    b. Modify those accounts via typing over the numbers.
7. Ensure Convergence.
    a. Choose CALC.
    b. If converged go to 8.
    c. If not converged repeat a.
8. View or Print Results.
    a. View via choosing OVERRIDE.
    b. Print via choosing PRINT.

TECHNICAL INFORMATION AND TEMPLATE LIMITATIONS
The template is limited to a minimum of two years and a maximum of five years of historical data. A three-year pro forma results.

RELATIONSHIP BETWEEN ASSUMPTIONS, OVERRIDE AND FORECAST (THIS SECTION IS OPTIONAL AND NOT NECESSARY FOR MOST USERS)
It may be helpful for some users to know more about the relationship between ASSUMPTIONS and OVERRIDE. This section is presented for this purpose and may be skipped by all but those who have an interest in this matter.

INITIAL RELATIONSHIPS
Prior to using either the ASSUMPTIONS or OVERRIDE options, a relationship exists between the historical data, the assumptions and the pro forma statements. The following describes this relationship:

   Historical data and assumptions
   The assumptions and the data calculated in this area of the spreadsheet represent the arithmetical averages of the various accounts based upon the historical statements. Thus, if three years of data have been entered and the company achieved 12% and 15% sales growth (on a year over year basis), 13.5% will be used to project sales growth for each of the years in the three year forecast period. Averages are similarly calculated for the other accounts in the assumptions block. (The historical summary that can be viewed with the ASSUMPTIONS menu choice actually shows much of the data used for Assumptions.)

   Assumptions and forecast
   The contents of the forecasted P&L and Balance Sheet are initially controlled by the Assumptions. The numbers in the assumptions section are spread across the income statement and balance sheet accounts using formulas built into the pro forma statement's cells. The bright cells in the forecasted statements are the cells that use the data from the assumptions section and convert it to numbers. These formulas generally represent an historical relationship of that asset to other assets in its class. In the case of current assets, for example, all current assets except cash and marketable securities are calculated from the "Other C.A. - %" (line 119) entry in the assumptions sheet. While this percentage (and the sales figure) determines the total of these accounts, the individual accounts in the forecasted balance sheet are based upon the historical relationships they have had with one another. In effect, if accounts receivable has averaged 52% of all non-cash current receivables in the past, it will represent 52% in the forecast.

BREAKING THE RELATIONSHIPS

When one chooses either ASSUMPTIONS or OVERRIDE and inputs data, the relationships described above are broken. Breaking the relationships is not necessarily bad, although it has implications for how the model works.

Assumptions

Typing in new data via the ASSUMPTIONS menu option severs the link between that cell and the historical data. It does not in any way affect the link between the assumptions and the forecasted data. That is, the data in the assumptions block, <u>whether calculated via the original formulas or input via user overtyping</u>, will still feed into the pro forma statements in the same manner. Of course, making a change in the assumptions will cause a change in the numbers in the pro forma statements (after re-calculating the spreadsheet), but <u>the manner in which the pro forma statements is affected by the assumption data is unchanged.</u>

Overriding the Pro Forma Statements

Using the OVERRIDE option and then "fine-tuning" the forecasted statements via overtyping some of the accounts severs the link between that cell and the assumptions. Because of this "unlinking," subsequent changes in the assumptions data may not flow through to the pro forma statements in the manner in which you expect them to. Thus, <u>the OVERRIDE option should be used last</u>, after you are sure that you have made all the assumptions changes necessary.

108 Computer Models in Finance

PROBLEM:
Part I: Project the next three years for the Happy Daze Company. Assume that the company has 2,000,000 shares of common stock outstanding.

Part II: Improve the gross profit estimate utilizing the ASSUMPTIONS menu option and calculate a new forecast.

SOLUTION:
Part I: Choose DATA. Select WORKFILE (assuming that Happy Daze financial statements are still in the workfile) or select OTHER and type XHAPPY <RET> when prompted for the file name. Choose ASSUMPTIONS. You will see an Historical Summary of key statistics. This information is shown below (it cannot all fit on the computer screen; use the right-arrow cursor key [the number 6 on the numbers keypad on the right-hand side of your keyboard] to see the right-most columns):

HISTORICAL RESULTS

FOR YEAR:	1989	1990	1991	1992	1993	AVERAGE
Revenue - $	$33,000	$35,893	$42,555	$52,108	$62,319	$45,175
Sales Inc. -%	0.00%	8.77%	18.56%	22.45%	19.60%	17.34%
GM - %	30.78%	32.00%	29.57%	26.28%	23.43%	28.41%
SG&A - $	$6,354	$7,239	$7,939	$9,035	$9,765	$8,066
SG&A - %	19.25%	20.17%	18.66%	17.34%	15.67%	18.22%
Other I/(E) - %	0.00%	0.00%	0.00%	0.00%	0.00%	0.00%
Tax Rate -%	35.33%	34.23%	33.69%	30.99%	31.64%	33.18%
Cash	$422	$1,481	$1,281	$1,247	$1,532	$1,193
Other C.A. - %	28.83%	25.18%	24.83%	25.62%	24.74%	25.84%
Net Property	$5,995	$6,100	$7,900	$10,100	$13,421	$8,703
Net Property-%	18.17%	16.99%	18.56%	19.38%	21.54%	18.93%
Other Assets	$1,550	$2,070	$1,934	$1,934	$2,134	$1,924
Non-debt C.L.	14.16%	10.40%	10.39%	11.92%	12.91%	11.95%
Other Liab.	$250	$150	$243	$231	$307	$236
Other Liab -%	0.76%	0.42%	0.57%	0.44%	0.49%	0.54%
Div. per Share	$0.10	$0.15	$0.20	$0.20	$0.20	$0.17
Div. Payout-%	9.35%	12.20%	14.39%	13.79%	14.08%	12.76%

You can move to the ASSUMPTIONS section with several presses of the down-arrow key or one press of the END key. By using the cursor-movement keys, you will be able to move around within the ASSUMPTIONS and also back to the HISTORICAL RESULTS area. (The "Home" and "End" keys may also be used.) Move to line 126 and input 2000 for each year of the forecast (note that 2000 rather than 2000000 must be used because the scale is in thousands). Press <RET> and then select the CALC option to force convergence. After two selections of CALC, the statements have converged. (They actually converged during the first selection; however it is always safe to select too many times rather than too few.) Choose the OVERRIDE or PRINT option to see the pro forma income statement (Exhibit XXI-1) and the pro forma balance sheet (Exhibit XXI-2).

EXHIBIT XXI-1

HAPPY DAZE
PRO FORMA STATEMENTS

FOR YEARS:	1994	1995	1996
REVENUES	$73,127	$85,809	$100,691
Cost of Sales	$52,349	$61,428	$72,082
GROSS MARGIN	$20,778	$24,381	$28,610
Selling	$6,894	$8,090	$9,493
Administrative	$5,135	$6,025	$7,070
Other	$1,293	$1,517	$1,780
TOTAL SG&A	$13,322	$15,632	$18,343
OPERATING INC.	$7,456	$8,749	$10,266
Interest Exp.	$604	$587	$552
PRE-TAX INCOME	$6,852	$8,162	$9,714
Income Taxes	$2,273	$2,708	$3,223
NET PROFIT	$4,579	$5,454	$6,491
EPS	$2.29	$2.73	$3.25
Div/Share	$0.20	$0.20	$0.20

EXHIBIT XXI-2

HAPPY DAZE
PRO FORMA STATEMENTS

FOR YEARS:	1994	1995	1996
CURRENT ASSETS:			
Cash	$1,193	$1,193	$1,193
Mkt. Securities	$0	$90	$664
Accts. Rec.	$8,475	$9,945	$11,670
Inventories	$8,941	$10,492	$12,311
Other Current	$1,479	$1,736	$2,037
TOTAL CURRENT	$20,088	$23,456	$27,875
NET PROPERTY	$13,842	$16,243	$19,060
OTHER ASSETS	$3,115	$3,655	$4,289
TOTAL	$37,045	$43,354	$51,224
CURR. LIAB.:			
Accounts Pay.	$6,651	$7,804	$9,158
Accr. Liab.	$2,091	$2,454	$2,880
Notes Payable	$262	$0	$0
S.T. Debt	$212	$212	$212
TOTAL CURRENT	$9,216	$10,470	$12,249
LONG-TERM DEBT			
Notes Payable	$600	$600	$600
Bonds	$4,000	$4,000	$4,000
Bank Debt	$800	$800	$800
TOTAL L.T. DEBT	$5,400	$5,400	$5,400
OTHER LIAB.:			
Def. Inc. Tax	$307	$307	$307
TOTAL OTHER	$307	$307	$307
EQUITY:			
Common Stock	$1,200	$1,200	$1,200
Capital Surplus	$2,150	$2,150	$2,150
Ret. Earnings	$18,773	$23,826	$29,918
TOTAL EQUITY	$22,123	$27,176	$33,268
TOTAL	$37,045	$43,354	$51,224

Part II:
Choose ASSUMPTIONS. By reviewing the historical results and the assumptions, it should be apparent that the model uses the historical averages (in this case, five-year averages) as the basis for its assumptions. It is this mechanical forecasting, necessary for simple computer models such as this, that creates opportunities for refinements by thoughtful users. In this case, the use of averages ignores trends in the data.

A pronounced trend is the deterioration in the gross margin as a percentage of sales. From HISTORICAL RESULTS, the percentages over time are as follows:

FOR YEAR:	1989	1990	1991	1992	1993	AVERAGE
GM - %	30.78%	32.00%	29.57%	26.28%	23.43%	28.41%

The forecast, however, assumes that the gross margin percentage will be 28.41% of sales for all three years. Given the historical pattern, it is unlikely that a rather steady decline down to 23.43% in 1993 would dramatically reverse itself by an improvement of almost 5 percentage points in 1996. If we believed that an improvement would take place, it might be more realistic to forecast a gradual return to higher gross margins. For purposes of seeing how a user might modify the assumptions, change the gross margin percentages to the following:

ASSUMPTIONS:	1994	1995	1996
GM - %	------------	25.00%	26.50%	28.00%

These changes are made by typing over the 28.41% on line 113 with the above information.

If there were other assumptions to be changed, they would be made in the same manner. When finished, merely type <RET>. An automatic recalculation of the data is done, and the user returns to the template menu.

After pressing the CALC key to recalculate three more times, the revised pro forma income statement (Exhibit XXI-3) and balance sheet (Exhibit XXI-4) is calculated. The results are shown below.

EXHIBIT XXI-3

HAPPY DAZE
PRO FORMA STATEMENTS

FOR YEARS:	1994	1995	1996
REVENUES	$73,127	$85,809	$100,691
Cost of Sales	$54,845	$63,070	$72,498
GROSS MARGIN	$18,282	$22,739	$28,194
Selling	$6,894	$8,090	$9,493
Administrative	$5,135	$6,025	$7,070
Other	$1,293	$1,517	$1,780
TOTAL SG&A	$13,322	$15,632	$18,343
OPERATING INC.	$4,960	$7,107	$9,850
Interest Exp.	$691	$760	$846
PRE-TAX INCOME	$4,269	$6,347	$9,004
Income Taxes	$1,416	$2,106	$2,987
NET PROFIT	$2,853	$4,242	$6,017
EPS	$1.43	$2.12	$3.01
Div/Share	$0.20	$0.20	$0.20

EXHIBIT XXI-4

HAPPY DAZE
PRO FORMA STATEMENTS

FOR YEARS:	1994	1995	1996
CURRENT ASSETS:			
Cash	$1,193	$1,193	$1,193
Accts. Rec.	$8,475	$9,945	$11,670
Inventories	$8,941	$10,492	$12,311
Other Current	$1,479	$1,736	$2,037
TOTAL CURRENT	$20,088	$23,365	$27,211
NET PROPERTY	$13,842	$16,243	$19,060
OTHER ASSETS	$3,115	$3,655	$4,289
TOTAL	$37,045	$43,263	$50,560
CURR. LIAB.:			
Accounts Pay.	$6,651	$7,804	$9,158
Accr. Liab.	$2,091	$2,454	$2,880
Notes Payable	$1,987	$2,848	$2,748
S.T. Debt	$212	$212	$212
TOTAL CURRENT	$10,941	$13,318	$14,997
LONG-TERM DEBT			
Notes Payable	$600	$600	$600
Bonds	$4,000	$4,000	$4,000
Bank Debt	$800	$800	$800
TOTAL L.T. DEBT	$5,400	$5,400	$5,400
OTHER LIAB.:			
Def. Inc. Tax	$307	$307	$307
TOTAL OTHER	$307	$307	$307
EQUITY:			
Common Stock	$1,200	$1,200	$1,200
Capital Surplus	$2,150	$2,150	$2,150
Ret. Earnings	$17,047	$20,888	$26,505
TOTAL EQUITY	$20,397	$24,238	$29,855
TOTAL	$37,045	$43,263	$50,560

(SEE NEXT PAGE FOR ADDITIONAL INFORMATION ON OVERRIDE)

A VERBAL EXAMPLE OF USING OVERRIDE

If one has made all of the changes in the assumptions that are deemed necessary, it is at this point that "fine-tuning" via the OVERRIDE option would be used. The following discussion suggests how this option might be used.

In reviewing the data from Exhibit XXI-4, suppose you felt that the inventory balances were too high because the company was planning to streamline its product line and also implement a better inventory control system. Because the assumption's approach has only carried the historical performance forward, the following forecasted inventory balances must be altered:

Original Forecast $8,941 $10,492 $12,311

Instead of these balances, a better estimate of would be: $8,500, $9,750, and $11,000, respectively. In order to make these changes, select OVERRIDE, go to the cells and type over the original forecast with the figures above. CALC until convergence. (No output is shown for this solution.)

This is a typical use of OVERRIDE. Some observations regarding this inventory discussion may be useful. First, OVERRIDE was used after all assumption changes were made. Second, the OVERRIDE change required another CALC to activate the convergence process. Third, the inventory modifications could have been achieved via the ASSUMPTIONS menu option (although not nearly as easily). It is this third point that requires some commentary because it may provide the user with some additional insights into the relationship between the ASSUMPTIONS and OVERRIDE menu options and when to use one versus the other.

To achieve the inventory numbers via the ASSUMPTIONS option, one would have modified (via a "guessing" approach) the percentages in line 119, "Other C.A. - %". After some trial and error, one would have duplicated (or very closely approximated) the desired inventory figures. However, this line controls all of the other current asset accounts except cash and marketable securities. Changes made in line 119 would produce changes in accounts receivable and other current asset accounts. These changes were not wanted. Thus, a user would end up, had he chosen this approach, having to make modifications using OVERRIDE to the accounts receivable and other affected current accounts. The use of ASSUMPTIONS, while mechanically possible, is more tedious.

PART VI:
FORECASTING

CHAPTER	TOPIC	NAME	PAGE
21	Pro Forma Statements	PLAN	103
22	Cash Budgeting	CASHBUD	121
23	Sustainable Growth	GROWTH	131

Part VI deals with forecasting. There are three models devoted to forecasting:

PLAN - Model is written up in previous section of the book, Part V: Statement Analysis. It is accessible from software from either FORECASTING or STATEMENT ANALYSIS. Refer to Chapter 21 for the write-up of this model.

CASHBUD - A monthly cash budgeting model. Provides a user with a great deal of flexibility regarding collections and payables and enables a forecast period of 24 months to be used.

GROWTH - A simple model to determine the maximum sales growth a company may have without having to go to the equity market.

Chapter 22 CASH BUDGETING

PURPOSE
To calculate monthly cash flows, cash balances, borrowing requirements, and cumulative new debt for a forecast period of up to 24 months.

LOADING THE TEMPLATE
From the FORECASTING sub-menu choose number: 1
From LOTUS choose file name: CASHBUD

TEMPLATE MENU
Menu choices available and their functions are as follows:

    OLD DATA - input data via overtyping existing data
    NEW DATA - erase existing data and input new data
    VIEW - view monthly cash flows
    GRAPH - output shown in graph form
    PRINT - prints cash budget (first 12 months or all 24 months
            depending upon the length of the forecast period)
    HELP - presents two help screens (To move from one to the
           other use the CURSOR MOVEMENT keys. To return to pro-
           cessing use <RET>.)
    END - allows the user to leave the cash budget template

HOW TO INPUT DATA
Choose OLD DATA menu option. (Unless you wish to erase the worksheet and start completely over, do not choose NEW DATA.) A submenu will appear and allow you to choose to input data in the upper portion of the template (UPPER DATA) or lower portion of the template (LOWER DATA). (The dichotomy for input ranges is made only to ease screen management during the input of data.) Choose either one and input data.

EXPLANATION OF CERTAIN INPUTS
<u>UPPER DATA</u>
A representation of the screen for the UPPER DATA input items is shown on the next page. The column of numbers on the left ranging from 3 to 24 represents the line numbers from the Lotus spreadsheet border and are referred to in the explanations that follow the screen representation.

118 Computer Models in Finance

```
              UPPER DATA SCREEN REPRESENTATION
-----------------------------------------------------------------
      3                 Collections        Payments
      4            |---------------|------------|
      5    Month  0 >   20.00%  ******     0.00%<
      6    Month +1 >   70.00%  ******   100.00%<
      7    Month +2 >   10.00%  ******          <
      8    Month +3 >           ******          <
      9    *************************************************
     10    TOTAL    *  100.00%  ******   100.00% ********
     11    *************************************************
     12    Disc - % >           ******          <
     13    % Taken  >           ******          <
     14    Purchases as % of Sales      >  60.00%<
     15    Purchases - mos. in advance  >      1 <
     16    PRIOR MONTH'S SALES*******************<PRIOR MONTH'S PURCHASES
     17    Month -1 ********* >     600 <          360 CAUTION
     18    Month -2 ********* >     500 <          360 CAUTION
     19    Month -3 ********* >         <          300 CAUTION
     20    ***********************************************
     21    Beginning Cash *********** >      50 <
     22    Minimum Cash  ************* >      50 <
     23    Number of Months*********** >       3 <
-----------------------------------------------------------------
```

Collections/Payments (Lines 5-8) - Represents the percentage collected/paid of current months sales/purchases during current month and the next three months.

THE SUM OF BOTH THESE COLUMNS MUST TOTAL 100%.

Line 10 is not an input line and will not calculate until the entire spreadsheet calculates. If the totals are not equal to 100%, you will be alerted by the program when it calculates or when you choose the VIEW or PRINT options. For example, the data above has 20% of sales this month, collected this month, 70% next month and 10% two months from now. For purchases made this month, nothing is paid. All payments (100%) are made the month after purchase. (NOTE: business problems where the company changes assumptions for future collections/payments must be handled carefully. See the PROBLEM and SOLUTION sections below for an example of such a situation. Page 130, in particular, is helpful for understanding how to handle such situations.)

Disc - % (Line 12) - Represents cash discounts offered to
    customers or offered by suppliers. If the company offers a
    2% discount to its customers, 2% would be entered in the
    left-hand (Collections) column. If suppliers offer a 2% dis-
    count to the company, 2% would be entered in the right-hand
    (Payments) column. In the screen representation above, no
    discounts were offered or available so the input range is
    left blank. (entering zeros would work just as well.) Disc -
    % (Line 12) and % Taken (Line 13) work together.(See part C
    of sample problem for example that involves both Line 12 and
    13)

% Taken (Line 13) - Represents the proportion of discounts from
    Line 12 taken by customers/company. In the example above,
    where no discounts were present in the problem, this line
    has no meaning. (See part C of sample problem for example
    that involves both Lines 12 and 13)

Purchases as % of Sales (Line 14) - Represents the relationship
    between purchases and sales. In the data above, purchases
    equal to 60% of sales are assumed.

Purchases - mos. in advance (Line 15) - Represents the number of
    months in advance of sales that purchases are made. In the
    example above, purchases are made this month for next
    month's expected sales (From line 14, the amount purchased
    this month will equal 60% of next month's sales.) IMPORTANT:
    The entry on Line 15 must be either 0, 1 or 2.

Prior Month's Sales/Prior Month's Purchases (Lines 17 - 19) -
    These lines represent sales/purchases that have occurred
    prior to the forecast period. In the data above, sales a
    month ago were 600 and two months ago were 500. This data
    was input by the user. Prior Month's Purchases were not in-
    put by the user but were calculated by the program. The data
    shows results from calculations made from Purchases as % of
    Sales (Line 14), Purchases - mos. in advance (Line 15) and
    the various sales input by the user. If necessary, the user
    may type directly (or overtype the entries) into the Prior
    Month's Purchases column. However, OVERTYPING WILL DESTROY
    THE FORMULAS IN THESE CELLS and subsequent automatic cal-
    culation of these three items will not be made. (Choosing
    the NEW DATA option from the TEMPLATE MENU will erase all
    data and restore the formulas in these cells, as will
    "rebooting" the CASHBUD template.) Depending upon the par-
    ticular problem at hand, it may be necessary to input data
    directly into these cells. (See LOWER DATA "DISBURSED Oth
    Purch - Line 48" below for another way to handle prior
    month's purchases without disrupting the formulas in this
    section of the worksheet.)

120 Computer Models in Finance

LOWER DATA
Data to be input (and the corresponding line number in the Lotus model) in the lower portion of the screen are the following:

SALES (Line 29) - Sales may be input two ways: individually or "automatically."
    <u>Individual</u> monthly entries are made by moving the cursor to the month and typing in the sales for that month. This is the entry method called for by most problems and business situations.
    "<u>Automatic</u>" entry is made by only entering the first month's sales. If the growth percentage is 0%, then the first month's sales will automatically (after CALCULATION of the template) be input for all subsequent months. (A non-zero entry will cause sales to increase or decrease by that percentage in each subsequent month. This entry is also automatic.)
    CAUTION: Individual monthly entries eliminates (via erasing the formula in the cell) the ability to have "automatic" processing work for that month.

PURCHASES (Line 30) - Purchases may be "automatically" calculated or input individually.
    "<u>Automatic</u>" entry requires no input to any item on line 30. That is, just skip the line entirely and proceed to lower level entry lines. This is the entry method called for by most problems and business situations.
    <u>Individual</u> entry involves moving to the particular cell and typing in the purchases for that month. This method is not encouraged although may be necessary in some situations.
    CAUTION: Using this method eliminates future "automatic" processing in the months that are individually input. (Even where it is necessary to abandon the fixed relationship between sales and purchases, it may be advantageous to utilize the DISBURSED - Oth Purch [line 48] input area discussed below.)

REVENUE - Other (Line 38) - This input line is provided for extraordinary or non-sales types of collections. Items must be entered individually for the months required.

DISBURSED - Oth Purch (Line 48) - This line is provided for extraordinary purchases or purchases that are not tied directly to sales. It may be used in a manner to avoid entries (and the destruction of cell formulas that results from such entries) in PRIOR MONTH'S PURCHASES (Lines 17 - 19) or PURCHASES (Line 30).

Lines 51 - 55 are expense or other items requiring individual monthly entries.

CALCULATING THE RESULTS
While entering data, press <RET> without entering a number. Calculation will be performed automatically by the program. The program will return to the TEMPLATE MENU after calculation is complete. IMPORTANT: Do not use the LOTUS <F9> key to calculate.

TECHNICAL INFORMATION AND TEMPLATE LIMITATIONS
The cash budgeting template is limited to a 24 month forecast. The print option will print the first 12 months of data or all 24 months of data. If the forecast exceeds 12 months, then all 24 months will be printed. Otherwise, 12 months are printed.

PROBLEM
Sport Uniforms, Inc. supplies baseball and basketball uniforms to sporting goods distributors. The company has a seasonal business with Spring and Fall peaks. All sales are for credit, and the company collects 20 percent of its sales during the month of the sale, 70 percent in the subsequent month, and 10 percent two months after the sale. Purchases are received in the month prior to the sale and equal 60 percent of sales in the subsequent month. Payments are made a month after the purchase is received. Administrative costs are expected to be $140 in February, $210 in March, and $170 in April. Other cash outlays are expected to be $120 per month for February through April. Actual (A) and forecasted (F) sales for December through May are as follows:

Dec. (A)	$ 500		Feb. (F)	800		Apr. (F)	900
Jan. (A)	600		Mar. (F)	1,100		May (F)	800

At the end of January, Sport Uniforms, Inc. had $100 of cash.

1. Prepare a monthly cash budget for the months of February through April assuming that the minimum cash balance required each month is $100. Determine the amount of new borrowing required each month and the cumulative new debt by month.

2. Sport Uniforms, Inc.'s controller has determined that bank borrowing can be reduced by slowing down payables to suppliers and enticing customers to pay faster with a 2% cash discount. He estimates that only 50% of his suppliers must be paid in the month subsequent to purchase, and the remainder can be "stretched" to the following month. (Because he has not yet sent out the payments for January [for purchases received in December], he can receive the benefits from this action immediately.) He estimates that offering a 2% cash discount to customers will increase the amount paying in the current month to 40% and decrease the amount paying in the second month to 50%. If 30% of the customers take advantage of the discount and he implements the "stretch" in payables, what will the effect be on cash flows? What will the discounts cost the company per month?

122 Computer Models in Finance

SOLUTION

SOLUTION TO PART 1.
Choose the OLD DATA option and UPPER DATA. Enter the following data (numbers to the left refer to line numbers in template):

Line
Number

```
    3                   Collections       Payments
    4             |---------------|------------|
    5     Month  0 >      20.00%  ******    0.00%<
    6     Month +1 >      70.00%  ******  100.00%<
    7     Month +2 >      10.00%  ******         <
    8     Month +3 >              ******         <
    9     *************************************************
   10     TOTAL    *     100.00%  ******  100.00% ********
   11     *************************************************
   12     Disc - % >              ******         <
   13     % Taken  >              ******         <
   14     Purchases as % of Sales      >    60.00%<
   15     Purchases - mos. in advance  >        1 <
   16     PRIOR MONTH'S SALES *****************<
   17     Month -1 ********* >       600 <
   18     Month -2 ********* >       500 <
   19     Month -3 ********* >           <
   20     *************************************************
   21     Beginning Cash *********** >       100 <
   22     Minimum Cash ************* >       100 <
   23     Number of Months*********** >        3 <
   24     ----------------------------------------
```

   NOTE that no PRIOR MONTH'S PURCHASES were entered! They will be "automatically" calculated and used when the spreadsheet is calculated.

Type <RET> to return to the TEMPLATE MENU, and then select OLD DATA and input the LOWER DATA items. In brief, the entries required in this section are the following:

   SALES (Line 29) must be input individually.
   PURCHASES No entry should be made to PURCHASES (Line 30). They will automatically be calculated by the program.
   ADMIN. EXP. and OTHER should be entered on Lines 52 and 54.

Exhibit XXII-1 on the next page shows the results.

EXHIBIT XXII-1

SPORT UNIFORMS, INC.
PART 1. CASH BUDGET

```
---------------------------------------------------------------
25  MONTHLY CASH BUDGET     Feb.    March   April
26  =========================================================
27  MONTHS:        Growth      1        2        3        4
28  ---------------------------------------------------------------
29  SALES          0.00%     800     1100      900      800
30  PURCHASES      NA        660      540      480      480
31
32  REVENUE:
33  Coll.Mo. -3                0        0        0        0
34  Coll.Mo. -2               50       60       80      110
35  Coll.Mo. -1              420      560      770      630
36  Coll.Mo.  0              160      220      180      160
37  Discounts                  0        0        0        0
38  Other                      0        0        0        0
39  ---------------------------------------------------------------
40  RECEIPTS                 630      840     1030       NA
41  ---------------------------------------------------------------
42  DISBURSED:
43  Purch. -3                  0        0        0        0
44  Purch. -2                  0        0        0        0
45  Purch. -1                480      660      540      480
46  Purch.  0                  0        0        0        0
47  Discounts                  0        0        0        0
48  Oth Purch                  0        0        0        0
49  ---------------------------------------------------------------
50  PURCHASES                480      660      540       NA
51  PAYROLL
52  ADMIN. EXP.              140      210      170
53  TAXES
54  OTHER                    120      120      120
55  CAPIT EXP.
56  ---------------------------------------------------------------
57  DISB'MENTS               740      990      830       NA
58  ---------------------------------------------------------------
59  NET CASH                -110     -150      200       NA
60  =========================================================
61  CASH BALANCE:
62  BEG. CASH:               100      100      100      100
63  END CASH                 -10      -50      300       NA
64  MINIMUM BAL              100      100      100      100
65  ---------------------------------------------------------------
66  BORROW                   110      150        0       NA
67  PAYDOWN                    0        0      200       NA
68  NEW DEBT                 110      260       60       NA
```

124 Computer Models in Finance

INTERPRETATION OF SOLUTION TO PART 1:
The forecasted net effect on cash each month is shown on line 59. Sport Uniforms, Inc.'s disbursements exceed receipts for the first two months (February and March) by $110 and $150, respectively. In April, receipts exceed disbursements by $200.

Line 66 represents the amount of borrowing required each month. Line 67 represents the amount used to pay down loans. Line 68 is a cumulative summary of the <u>new</u> debt (i.e., additional debt needed during the forecast period). For Part 1, new debt peaks at $260 in March. By the end of the forecast period, new debt is $60 higher than the beginning of the forecast period.

SOLUTION TO PART 2.
Choose the OLD DATA option because much of the Part 1 data is relevant to Part 2. Choose the UPPER DATA option. The data remain the same as before except for the items shown underlined below (line numbers are provided merely for reference):

Line Number		Collections		Payments	
5	Month 0 >	<u>40.00%</u>	******	0.00%	<
6	Month +1 >	<u>50.00%</u>	******	<u>50.00%</u>	<
7	Month +2 >	10.00%	******	<u>50.00%</u>	<
12	Disc - % >	2.00%	******		<
13	% Taken >	30.00%	******		<

The three underlined amounts on lines 5 and 6 indicate new data entries that were typed over existing data. The other three underlined items (on lines 7, 12 and 13) were typed in cells that previously did not contain data.

One data change must be made in the LOWER DATA area. In line 38, REVENUE - Other, input 120 for month 1 (see "Explanation of Line 38" on page 130 for information regarding this entry).

The changes recommended by the controller produce the results shown in Exhibit XXII-2 on the next page.

Manually insert $120 in line 38

Chapter 22: Cash Budgeting   **125**

EXHIBIT XXII-2

SPORT UNIFORMS, INC.
PART 2. CASH BUDGET

```
----------------------------------------------------------------
25  MONTHLY CASH BUDGET
26  ================================================================
27  MONTHS:      Growth        1        2        3        4
28  ----------------------------------------------------------------
29  SALES         0.00%       800     1100      900      800
30  PURCHASES       NA        660      540      480      480
31
32  REVENUE:
33  Coll.Mo. -3                 0        0        0        0
34  Coll.Mo. -2                50       60       80      110
35  Coll.Mo. -1               300      400      550      450
36  Coll.Mo.  0               320      440      360      320
37  Discounts                  -5       -7       -5       -5
38  Other                    (120)      0        0        0
39  ----------------------------------------------------------------
40  RECEIPTS                  785      893      985       NA
41  ----------------------------------------------------------------
42  DISBURSED:
43  Purch. -3                   0        0        0        0
44  Purch. -2                 180      240      330      270
45  Purch. -1                 240      330      270      240
46  Purch.  0                   0        0        0        0
47  Discounts                   0        0        0        0
48  Oth Purch                   0        0        0        0
49  ----------------------------------------------------------------
50  PURCHASES                 420      570      600       NA
51  PAYROLL
52  ADMIN. EXP.               140      210      170
53  TAXES
54  OTHER                     120      120      120
55  CAPIT EXP.
56  ----------------------------------------------------------------
57  DISB'MENTS                680      900      890       NA
58  ----------------------------------------------------------------
59  NET CASH                  105       -7       95       NA
60  ================================================================
61  CASH BALANCE:
62  BEG. CASH:                100      205      199      293
63  END CASH                  205      199      293       NA
64  MINIMUM BAL               100      100      100      100
65  ----------------------------------------------------------------
66  BORROW                      0        0        0       NA
67  PAYDOWN                     0        0        0       NA
68  NEW DEBT                    0        0        0       NA
```

INTERPRETATION OF SOLUTION TO PART 2:
The controller's actions cause a significant improvement in the short-term cash flows of the company. There is no need to borrow any funds during the forecast period. The cash balance at the end of the forecast period is $293 with no debt, compared to $100 with $60 debt in the prior scenario. The cost of the cash discount is clearly shown on line 37, running about $5 per month except for March when it is $7.

EXPLANATION OF LINE 38
Because the new credit terms do not affect past sales or receivables, existing receivables at the time of the switch are expected to be collected based upon prior experience. The CASHBUD template, however, cannot automatically deal with such "switch-overs" which necessitates special entries by the user (see below for method). In this instance, only the payment percentages of the current month and one month after the sale have changed (2 months after remained the same). Based on this change, only sales last month, January, must be adjusted for the collections during the first month of the new policy. 70% of these sales can be expected to be collected during month 1. Yet the new input "forces" a 50% amount into line 35 (Coll. Mo. -1). We can overtype the amount in this cell (300 after calculation) with the old amount ($420) from Part 1, or we can input the difference into line 38. Ignoring this adjustment is to assume that a large portion of receivables ($120) from January are never collected.

SUPPLEMENTARY COMMENT ON "SWITCH-OVER" PROBLEMS
"Switch-over" situations are common in business. Companies are frequently faced with liquidity problems that they try to solve by (temporarily) using vendor "stretch."

Had Part 2. of the problem included data that changed other percentages in the collection input range, the adjustment would have been more complex but not overly difficult to handle. A general framework for handling all of these "switch-over" situations follows:

1. Calculate the cash flows under the old collection assumptions.
2. Calculate the cash flows under the new collection assumptions.
3. Determine which of the new collection assumptions cause "switch-over" problems.
    a. These will depend on the particular situation.
    b. They cannot affect more than the first 3 months.
4. Determine the difference between the new and the old for the affected ("switch-over") collections. (Note these can only affect months 1-3.)
5. Input the differences on line 38.
6. Recalculate the template to obtain the correct results.

Chapter 23 SUSTAINABLE GROWTH

PURPOSE: To determine the maximum sales dollar growth rate for a firm using no outside equity financing.

LOADING THE TEMPLATE
From the FORECASTING sub-menu choose number: 3
From LOTUS choose file name: GROWTH

TEMPLATE MENU: Menu choices available are as follows:
   DATA - input data
   END - allows the user to leave this template

HOW TO INPUT DATA: Choose DATA menu option. Cursor will move to the first input field. (Note that input fields are generally shown on the screen between ">" and "<" symbols.) Input for this template is in the range of cells C3 - C6.

EXPLANATION OF CERTAIN INPUTS
"Spontaneous Liabilities," while not a direct input, is a definition that must be known to properly handle the inputs. Spontaneous liabilities are those liabilities that vary directly with sales. These are generally current liabilities. The most common spontaneous liabilities are accounts payable and accrued expenses. (NOTE: not all current liabilities are spontaneous.)

   ROS - Net Profit/Sales
   Turnover - Sales/Capital
      where Capital = Total Assets - Spontaneous Liabilities
   D/E - Non-Spontaneous Liabilities/Equity
   Payout - Percentage of Earnings Paid out as Dividends

CALCULATING THE RESULTS
While entering data, press <RET> without entering a number. Calculation will be performed automatically by the program. The program will return to the TEMPLATE MENU after calculation is complete. IMPORTANT: Do not use the LOTUS <F9> key to calculate.

TECHNICAL INFORMATION AND TEMPLATE LIMITATIONS
Sustainable growth models are quick and less than perfect substitutes for doing pro forma statements. They tend to be simplistic because of the restrictive assumptions. The following assumptions are built into this model:

   i. total assets vary with sales
   ii. liabilities vary with sales
   iii. liabilities maintain a constant proportion to equity

The formula used to calculate sustainable growth is as follows:

G = M*(1-P)*(1+L)/(A - M*(1-P)*(1+L))

where

> G = sustainable growth in dollar sales expressed as a percentage
>
> M = net profit margin   (earnings/sales)
>
> P = payout ratio   (dividends/earnings)
>
> 1-P = 1 - payout ratio or the retention ratio
>
> L = 1 + modified debt/equity ratio where the numerator of the modified debt/equity ratio is total liabilities - spontaneous liabilities
>
> A = reciprocal of modified turnover ratio where the modified turnover ratio is sales/(assets - spontaneous liabilities)

PROBLEM:

Solve parts I and II below.

Part I:
Assume the Fancy Gap Company is willing to utilize debt (excluding spontaneous liabilities) up to 50 percent of its equity. If assets will be 75 percent of sales, spontaneous liabilities will be 15 percent of sales, and the company plans to pay dividends equal to 25 percent of earnings, how fast can sales grow if Fancy Gap has a profit margin (return on sales) of 5%?

Part II:
How fast could Fancy Gap grow if it lowered its payout to 0% (i.e. it stopped paying dividends)? How fast if it raised the payout ratio to 50% (i.e. doubled the dividend)?

SOLUTION:

Part I:
Select the DATA option and input the information. Fancy Gap will be able to grow at up to a 10.37% sales growth rate without requiring outside equity. The correct inputs and solution are shown below:

```
    <ALT> B to Restart          SUSTAINABLE GROWTH
===============================================================
ROS        >        5.00%   < Net Profit/Sales
Turnover   >        1.67    < Sales/Capital
D/E        >       50.00%   < Non-Spontaneous Liabilities/Equity
Payout     >       25.00%   < % Earnings Paid out as Dividends
===============================================================
           SOLUTION:         10.37%   Sustainable Growth Rate
===============================================================
```

Part II:

(a) Select DATA, overtype Payout with 0. Answer (not shown) is 14.32%.

(b) Select DATA overtype Payout with .5. Answer (not shown) is 6.68%.

PART VII:
CAPITAL BUDGETING

CHAPTER	TOPIC	NAME	PAGE
24	Capital Budgeting	CAPBUD	137
25	Lease-Buy Analysis	LEASEBUY	149

Part VII deals with capital budgeting techniques. Two models are included in this section:

CAPBUD - Assists in the evaluation of investment projects. The model handles either new or replacement projects. Annual projections of income and cash flow are developed and used in NPV, Present Value Index, Payback and IRR calculations.

LEASEBUY - Uses capital budgeting techniques to make the financial decision of whether to lease or buy an asset. Although technically a financing decision rather than an investment decision, the similarity in technique explains its reason for inclusion in this section. For software purposes, it is also menu accessible from the Financing sub-menu.

Chapter 24 CAPITAL BUDGETING

PURPOSE
To assist in the evaluation of investment projects. The model handles either new or replacement projects. Annual projections of income and cash flow are developed and used to calculate NPV, Present Value Index, Payback and IRR calculations.

LOADING THE TEMPLATE
From the CAPITAL BUDGETING sub-menu choose number: 1
From LOTUS choose file name: CAPBUD

TEMPLATE MENU: Menu choices available and their functions are as follows:
   OLD DATA - input data via overtyping existing data
   NEW DATA - erase existing data and input new data
   VIEW - move around the spreadsheet to view output
   GRAPH - output shown in graph form
   PRINT - prints assumptions and analysis
   HELP - presents a help screen
   END - allows the user to leave this template

HOW TO INPUT DATA
Choose OLD DATA or NEW DATA menu option. Cursor will move to the first input field. (Note that input fields are generally shown on the screen between ">" and "<" symbols.) Input for this template is in the range of cells C4-C16, C19-C24, B28-L29 and B31-L32.

EXPLANATION OF CERTAIN INPUTS
The input is divided between NEW ASSET and OLD ASSET. OLD ASSET input should be used only when evaluating a replacement (e.g. the replacement of an existing machine with a new machine). Grouped by these two categories, the input items are as follows:

NEW ASSET (Cells C4-C16):
   Yr. 0 - The calendar year during which investment occurs
      (e.g., 1986)
   Cost of New Asset - Asset acquisition cost in dollars
   Installation Cost - Cost to install the asset
   Work'g Cap.-Init-$ - The increase or decrease in working capi-
      tal dollars required in time period 0. This amount also
      represents <u>the minimum</u> amount of working capital required
      during the life of the investment.
   Work'g Cap.-% Sales - A percentage entry that enables working
      capital dollars to vary directly with the revenue produced
      by the asset. It is applied to incremental sales (Sales
      from New Asset minus Sales from Old Asset) in the case of a
      replacement project.

   <u>NOTE THE RELATIONSHIP BETWEEN THE TWO WORKING CAPITAL
   ENTRIES:</u>
   The amount of working capital dollars assumed outstanding
   in any year is the <u>maximum</u> of the two entries. The cash
   flow associated with working capital is the change in working capital from the prior year.

Economic Life - The useful life of the asset in years (cannot exceed 10).
Est. Salvage Value - Expected pre-tax revenue from disposition of the asset at the end of its useful life.
Req'd Rate of Return - Percentage to be used for discounting. Usually the weighted-average cost of capital (WACC) or WACC adjusted for riskiness of asset.
Depreciation Life - The number of years to use for depreciation purposes. May be either longer or shorter than the economic life but cannot exceed 25 years. If MACRS depreciation method is chosen, this entry must be 3, 5, 7 or 10.
Deprec Method - Four depreciation methods are available. Enter the number of your choice: Straight-line = 1; Sum-of-years-digits = 2; 150% Declining Balance = 3; and MACRS = 4.
NOTE: If MACRS is chosen, Depreciation Life must be 3, 5, 7 or 10. (See TECHNICAL INFORMATION AND TEMPLATE LIMITATIONS below for additional information regarding depreciation.)
Sal. Value for Dep. - Value in dollars to be used for depreciation purposes. Does not have to equal the Est. Salvage Value above.
Capital Gains Rate % - The tax rate in % applicable to capital gains.
Marginal Tax Rate % - The tax rate in % applicable to ordinary income.

OLD ASSET (Cells C19-C24):
Original Cost - The purchase price plus installation cost.
Depreciation Life - The number of years chosen to depreciate the asset.
Depreciation Left - The number of full years of depreciation left.
ITC Recapture - Any recapture of Investment Tax Credit as a result of abandoning this asset.
Salvage Val. Now - Value if it is disposed of now.
Salvage Val. End - Value if one continued to operate the asset and disposed of it at the end of the New Asset life (a period of time equal to the economic life above).

NEW AND OLD ASSET (Lines 28, 29, 31 and 32)
In addition, there are New Asset revenue and expense lines (lines 28 and 29) and Old Asset revenue and expense lines (lines 31 and 32) for input. The following comments, while referencing the New Asset revenue and cash expense cells and lines <u>pertain equally to the corresponding Old Asset lines</u>.

Revenue - Expected sales revenue from the asset. The user has three distinct options regarding the input of revenues.
    OPTION ONE: If an entry is made in cell C28 only, then that revenue will be used for all years of the project.
    OPTION TWO: If a percentage is entered for "Growth" in cell B28, the revenue in cell C28 will grow each subsequent year by that percentage. (Leaving B28 blank or entering zero is equivalent to Option One and results in constant sales over the project life.)

OPTION THREE: The cursor can be moved to each of the future years (cells D28, E28 etc. to individually enter revenue figures for each year. **(See CAUTION below regarding Option Three)**

Cash Exp. - The dollars of cash expenses expected from the project. (Do not include depreciation expenses in this category!) The entry options discussed above for Revenue also pertain to Cash Exp.

INPUT CAUTION: Revenue and Cash Exp. entries may create a problem if Option Three is exercised. Typing entries into future years (cells to the right of C19 and C20) will destroy formulas embedded in those cells. If you choose this entry method and subsequently (without reloading this template) want to utilize either Options One or Two to perform sensitivity analysis, these options will not perform as described above. To avoid this problem, leave the Capital Budgeting template and then reload it. Reloading it restores the original formulas (although you will have to re-enter the data).

CALCULATING THE RESULTS
While entering data, press <RET> without entering a number. Calculation will be performed automatically by the program. The program will return to the TEMPLATE MENU after calculation is complete. IMPORTANT: Do not use the LOTUS <F9> key to calculate.

TECHNICAL INFORMATION AND TEMPLATE LIMITATIONS
The capital budgeting template is designed to handle new or replacement projects. Project life is limited to 10 years. All cash flows are assumed to occur at the end of each period. Investment (purchase cost and installation), initial working capital, ITC recapture and net salvage on old asset are assumed to occur in time period 0. No other flows occur in time period 0.

The 1986 Tax Act eliminated the Investment Tax Credit. Provision is made for ITC recapture on assets that are being replaced, although the user must calculate and input this information.

Depreciation methods and how they are handled in the template are as follows:
- Straight-line - The half-year convention is not used.
- MACRS - Only provision for 3, 5, 7 and 10 year lives are included in the model.
- SYD and 150% DB - both assume switch-over to straight-line.

For replacement assets:

The old asset is assumed to have used straight-line depreciation.

The old asset is assumed to have been usable for the life of the proposed new asset.

PROBLEMS

To adequately illustrate the use of this model, two problems are provided. The first is a new asset acquisition with three parts that help to demonstrate usage of the model. The second deals with a replacement asset.

PROBLEM 1 - NEW ASSET PROBLEM
Mr. Productmanager wants to produce kitchen sinks, a product his firm currently does not produce. To enter the field, he has determined it will cost $100,000 for a machine to produce kitchen sinks and $10,000 to install the machine. He estimates that the machine will have a 5 year useful life and produce revenues of $90,000 per year. The cash expenses to produce and sell the kitchen sinks are estimated to be $55,000 per year. The firm's relevant tax rate for ordinary income is 35%. The required return on this investment is 14%.

Part 1: Mr. Productmanager assumes 5-year straight-line depreciation and no salvage value after 5 years. What will the NPV, IRR, PVI and Payback be on this project?

Part 2: Mr. Bookmanager, the controller of the company, reviews Mr. Productmanager's assumptions and determines that Mr. Projectmanager could have used different assumptions to evaluate the project. He determines that the machine will be worth $10,000 at the end of 5 years and that MACRS depreciation should be used. What effect do these changes make in the analysis?

Part 3: Mr. Financemanager, the VP of Finance, suggests that Mr. Bookmanager's work, while an improvement over the original proposal of Mr. Productmanager, is still deficient. He argues that two key items have been left out of the analysis -- inflation and working capital requirements. Mr. Financemanager determines that an initial investment in inventory will be required in order to commence the production and selling of the new product. Further, once sales commence, funds will be tied up in accounts receivable. He determines that $4,000 will be required in order to start production and that working capital will average 10% of sales once selling commences. Regarding inflation, Mr. Financemanager knows that it has been incorporated into the market-determined 14% required rate of return but not into Mr. Productmanager's cash flows. After careful study, Mr. Financemanager determines that both revenues and cash expenses should grow at 5% per year due to inflation.

PROBLEM 2 - REPLACEMENT PROBLEM

ABC Company acquired a widget polishing machine 4 years ago. It cost $10,000 installed, and they chose to depreciate the machine using the straight-line method over 7 years. Recent changes in technology have produced new machines to perform the same function. One such machine costs $25,000 and is expected to reduce inventory requirements by $10,000 (working capital reduction) and annual operating cash expenses by $10,000 per year. The new machine is expected to last for 6 years, will be depreciated over 5 years via straight-line depreciation and is expected to have a salvage value of $2,000. If the company can sell the old machine for $3,000 now (it will be worthless 6 years from now), has a tax rate of 30% and a WACC of 15%, should the company replace the old machine?

SOLUTIONS

Problem 1: PART 1.
Choose the NEW DATA option. Enter the information as shown below:

CAPITAL BUDGETING ASSUMPTIONS

```
======================================
NEW ASSET INFORMATION:
Yr. 0 = (e.g. 1994) >        1994   <
Cost of New Asset    >    $100,000   <
Installation Cost    >     $10,000   <
Work'g Cap.-Init-$   >                <
Work'g Cap.-% Sales  >                <
Economic Life        >           5   <
Est. Salvage Value   >                <
Req'd Rate of Return>       14.00%   <
Depreciation Life    >           5   <
Deprec Method (1-4)  >           1   <
Sal. Value for Dep.  >                <
Capital Gains Rate %>                 <
Marginal Tax Rate %  >      35.00%   <

OLD ASSET INFORMATION:
Original Cost         >               <
Depreciation Life     >               <
Depreciation Left     >               <
ITC Recapture         >               <
Salvage Val. Now      >               <
Salvage Val. End      >               <
---------------------------------|------
                     Growth         1
---------------------------------|------------
NEW ASSET:
Revenue    >                     $90,000
Cash Exp.  >                     $55,000
OLD ASSET:
Revenue    >
Cash Exp.  >
---------------------------------------------
```

Press <RET> to calculate. The detailed cash flows and project summary statistics are shown in Exhibit XXIV-1. The specific information asked for in the problem is as follows:

IRR	11.91%	NPV	($5,463)
PAYBACK	3.61 yrs.	PVI	0.95

This information is obtained from the "CAPITAL BUDGETING PROJECT - SUMMARY STATISTICS," found below the detailed year-by-year cash flows (see EXHIBIT XXIV-1). The project, according to the discounted cash flow measures, should be rejected.

Problem 1: PART 2.
Choose the OLD DATA option, overtype Deprec Method with a 4 and enter 10,000 for Est. Salvage Value. Type <RET> to calculate. The results are shown in EXHIBIT XXIV-2. The changes made by Mr. Bookmanager were unable to make the project acceptable (NPV is still negative).

Problem 1: PART 3.
Choose OLD DATA option, enter Work'g Cap-Init-$ as 4000, Work'g Cap.-% Sales as .10 and .05 Growth for both Revenue and Cash Exp. The assumptions appear below.

CAPITAL BUDGETING ASSUMPTIONS

Yr. 0 = (e.g. 1986) >	1986 <
Cost of New Asset >	$100,000 <
Installation Cost >	$10,000 <
Work'g Cap.-Init-$ >	$4,000 <
Work'g Cap.-% Sales >	10.0%<
Economic Life >	5 <
Est. Salvage Value >	$10,000 <
Req'd Rate of Return >	14.00%<
Depreciation Life >	5 <
Deprec Method (1-4) >	4 <
Sal. Value for Dep. >	$0 <
Capital Gains Rate % >	<
Marginal Tax Rate % >	35.00%<

		Growth
NEW ASSET:		
Revenue >	5.00%	$90,000
Cash Exp. >	5.00%	$55,000

The detailed results are shown in EXHIBIT XXIV-3. The changes suggested by Mr. Financemanager both improve (incorporation of the inflation factor) and penalize (recognition of the effect of funds tied up in working capital) the cash flows. The net effect is to improve the discounted cash flow measures (IRR = 14.74% and NPV = $2,240) from Mr. Bookmanager's calculations. Based on these numbers, the project should be accepted.

EXHIBIT XXIV-1

PROBLEM 1

SOLUTION TO PART 1

MR. Productmanager'S CALCULATIONS

YEARS:	1994	1995	1996	1997	1998	1999
New Asset	$110,000					
Working Cap.	$0					
Old Asset	$0					
Tax on Sale	0					
ITC Recap.	0					
NET INVEST.	$110,000	$0	$0	$0	$0	$0
Net Revenue		$90,000	$90,000	$90,000	$90,000	$90,000
Net Expense		$55,000	$55,000	$55,000	$55,000	$55,000
Deprec - New		$22,000	$22,000	$22,000	$22,000	$22,000
Deprec - Old		0	0	0	0	0
GROSS INCOME		$13,000	$13,000	$13,000	$13,000	$13,000
Taxes		($4,550)	($4,550)	($4,550)	($4,550)	($4,550)
NET INCOME		$8,450	$8,450	$8,450	$8,450	$8,450
Depreciation		$22,000	$22,000	$22,000	$22,000	$22,000
Working Cap.		$0	$0	$0	$0	($0)
AT CF		$30,450	$30,450	$30,450	$30,450	$30,450
Salvage		$0	$0	$0	$0	$0
Tax on Salv.		$0	$0	$0	$0	$0
NET CASH	($110,000)	$30,450	$30,450	$30,450	$30,450	$30,450
CUM'L CASH	($110,000)	($79,550)	($49,100)	($18,650)	$11,800	$42,250
DISC. CASH	($110,000)	$26,711	$23,430	$20,553	$18,029	$15,815
DISC. CUM'L	($110,000)	($83,289)	($59,859)	($39,306)	($21,277)	($5,463)

```
CAPITAL BUDGETING PROJECT - SUMMARY STATISTICS
-----------------------------------------------
NET INV.    $110,000   DIS. RATE    14.00%
IRR           11.91%   NPV         ($5,463)
PAYBACK     3.61 yrs.  PVI            0.95
-----------------------------------------------
```

EXHIBIT XXIV-2

PROBLEM 1

SOLUTION TO PART 2

Mr. Bookmanager's CALCULATIONS

YEARS:	1994	1995	1996	1997	1998**
New Asset	$110,000				
Working Cap.	$0				
Old Asset	$0				
Tax on Sale	$0				
ITC Recap.	$0				
NET INVEST.	$110,000	$0	$0	$0	$0
Net Revenue		$90,000	$90,000	$90,000	$90,000
Net Expense		$55,000	$55,000	$55,000	$55,000
Deprec - New		$22,000	$35,200	$20,900	$13,200
Deprec - Old		$0	$0	$0	$0
GROSS INCOME		$13,000	($200)	$14,100	$21,800
Taxes		($4,550)	$70	($4,935)	($7,630)
NET INCOME		$8,450	($130)	$9,165	$14,170
Depreciation		$22,000	$35,200	$20,900	$13,200
Working Cap.		$0	$0	$0	$0
AT CF		$30,450	$35,070	$30,065	$27,370
Salvage		$0	$0	$0	$0
Tax on Salv.		$0	$0	$0	$0
NET CASH	($110,000)	$30,450	$35,070	$30,065	$27,370
CUM'L CASH	($110,000)	($79,550)	($44,480)	($14,415)	$12,955
DISC. CASH	($110,000)	$26,711	$26,985	$20,293	$16,205
DISC. CUM'L	($110,000)	($83,289)	($56,304)	($36,011)	($19,806)

CAPITAL BUDG

NET INV.	$110,000	DIS. RATE	14.00%
IRR	13.54%	NPV	($1,215)
PAYBACK	3.53 yrs.	PVI	0.99

** NOTE: 1999 Year not shown in this exhibit.

EXHIBIT XXIV-3

SOLUTION TO PART 3

Mr. Financemanager's CALCULATIONS

YEARS:	1994	1995	1996	1997	1998
Net Revenue		$90,000	$94,500	$99,225	$104,186
Net Expense		$55,000	$57,750	$60,638	$63,669
Deprec - New		$22,000	$35,200	$20,900	$13,200
Deprec - Old		$0	$0	$0	$0
GROSS INCOME		$13,000	$1,550	$17,688	$27,317
Taxes		($4,550)	($543)	($6,191)	($9,561)
NET INCOME		$8,450	$1,008	$11,497	$17,756
Depreciation		$22,000	$35,200	$20,900	$13,200
Working Cap.		$5,000	$450	$473	$496
AT CF		$25,450	$35,758	$31,924	$30,460
Salvage		$0	$0	$0	$0
Tax on Salv.		$0	$0	$0	$0
NET CASH	($114,000)	$25,450	$35,758	$31,924	$30,460
CUM'L CASH	($114,000)	($88,550)	($52,793)	($20,868)	$9,592
DISC. CASH	($114,000)	$22,325	$27,514	$21,548	$18,035
DISC. CUM'L	($114,000)	($91,675)	($64,161)	($42,613)	($24,578)

```
             CAPITAL BUDG
             -------------------------------------------
             NET INV.    $114,000    DIS. RATE    14.00%
             IRR           14.74%    NPV          $2,240
             PAYBACK     3.69 yrs.   PVI            1.02
             -------------------------------------------
```

** NOTE: 1999 Year not shown in this exhibit.

SOLUTION to Problem 2
Choose the NEW DATA option. The old data will be erased. Input the following information in the assumptions block:

Problem 2

ASSUMPTIONS
==
```
NEW ASSET INFORMATION:
Yr. 0 = (e.g. 1994)  >        1994    < Year to be Period 0
Cost of New Asset    >      $25,000   <
Installation Cost    >                <
Work'g Cap.-Init-$   >     ($10,000)  < Time 0 WC and Minimum WC
Work'g Cap.-% Sales  >                < Variable WC (with Sales)
Economic Life        >            6   < Life of Project (Max = 10)
Est. Salvage Value   >       $2,000   < Est. Disposal Value in Final
Year
Req'd Rate of Return >       15.00%   < Usually WACC
Depreciation Life    >            5   < If MACRS, must = 3,5,7 or 10
Deprec Method (1-4)  >            1   < 1=SL; 2=SYD;3=150%DB;4=MACRS
Sal. Value for Dep.  >                < For Deprec. Need not=Sal Val.
Capital Gains Rate % >                <
Marginal Tax Rate %  >       30.00%   <
```
~~~~~~
```
OLD ASSET INFORMATION:
Original Cost        >        10000   < Cost plus Installation
Depreciation Life    >            7   < Years of Depreciation
Depreciation Left    >            3   < Years of Depreciation Left
ITC Recapture        >                < Dollars of ITC Recaptured
Salvage Val. Now     >         3000   < Market Value Now
Salvage Val. End     >                < Market Value - end New Asset
                Growth            1
|------------------------------------
NEW ASSET:
Revenue       >
Cash Exp.     >
OLD ASSET:
Revenue       >
Cash Exp.     >          $10,000
------------------------------------------------------------
```

The last item, Cash Expense, is worth some comment. The problem says that the new machine will lower cash operating expenses by $10,000. That means that the old machine will have higher cash operating expenses than the new one by $10,000. Entering the data as above reflects this situation correctly. Another way of dealing with this type of differential would have been to enter a negative $10,000 in the NEW ASSET Cash Exp and a zero for OLD ASSET Cash Exp.

At this point, press <RET> without entering a number, and the solution shown in Exhibit XXIV-4 should result.

EXHIBIT XXIV-4

PROBLEM 2

```
-----------------------------------------------------------------
YEARS:              1994      1995      1996      1997      1998      1999
=================================================================
New Asset        $25,000
Working Cap.    ($10,000)
Old Asset         $3,000
Tax on Sale      ($1286)
ITC Recap.            0
                 -------------------------------------------------
NET INVEST.      $10,714        $0        $0        $0        $0        $0
-----------------------------------------------------------------


YEARS:        1994      1995      1996      1997      1998      1999      2000
=================================================================
Net Revenue        $0        $0        $0        $0        $0        $0
Net Expense  ($10,000) ($10,000) ($10,000) ($10,000) ($10,000) ($10,000)
Deprec - New   $5,000    $5,000    $5,000    $5,000    $5,000        $0
Deprec - Old   $1,429    $1,429    $1429         0         0         0
             ------------------------------------------------------
GROSS INCOME   $3,571    $3,571    $3,571    $5,000    $5,000   $10,000
Taxes         ($1,071)  ($1,071)  ($1,071)  ($1,500)  ($1,500)  ($3,000)
             ------------------------------------------------------
NET INCOME     $2,500    $2,500    $2,500    $3,500    $3,500    $7,000
Depreciation   $3,571    $3,571    $3,571    $5,000    $5,000        $0
Working Cap.  $10,000        $0        $0        $0        $0       ($0)
             ------------------------------------------------------
AT CF         ($3,929)   $6,071    $6,071    $8,500    $8,500    $7,000
Salvage            $0        $0        $0        $0        $0    $2,000
Tax on Salv.       $0        $0        $0        $0        $0     ($686)
             ------------------------------------------------------
NET     ($10,714) ($3,929)   $6,071    $6,071    $8,500    $8,500    $9,686
=================================================================
```

```
         CAPITAL BUDGETING PROJECT - SUMMARY STATISTICS
         ----------------------------------------
         NET INV.    $10,714  DIS. RATE   15.00%
         IRR          29.71%  NPV         $7,726
         PAYBACK    3.29 yrs. PVI           1.72
         ----------------------------------------
```

Chapter 25 LEASE-BUY ANALYSIS

PURPOSE: To evaluate a lease versus purchase alternative. The purchase is assumed to be financed with debt.

LOADING THE TEMPLATE
From the CAPITAL BUDGETING sub-menu choose number: 2
From LOTUS choose file name: LEASEBUY

TEMPLATE MENU
Menu choices available and their functions are as follows:
   OLD DATA - input data without erasing existing data
   NEW DATA - erase existing data and input new data
   VIEW -   view the lease-buy analysis
   PRINT - prints the assumptions and the lease-buy analysis
   HELP - presents a help screen
   END - allows the user to leave this template

HOW TO INPUT DATA
Choose OLD DATA or NEW DATA option from menu. Cursor will move to the first input field. (Note that input fields are generally shown on the screen between ">" and "<" symbols.) Input for this template is in the range of cells C3 - C15

EXPLANATION OF CERTAIN INPUTS
Timing of Payment - if the lease payments are made in advance
   (the beginning of the year), choose 0; if at the end of the
   year, choose 1.
Diff. Operating Cost - costs such as maintenance and repairs that
   are included in the lease contract but must be paid under
   the purchase option.
Depreciation Life or Method - See explanation in previous chapter
   on Capital Budgeting (CAPBUD)
Est. Salvage Val - estimated disposition value at the end of the
   useful life of the asset.
Borrowing Rate - interest rate paid on debt.
Higher Risk Rate - rate used to discount the salvage value to
   reflect higher uncertainty associated with this estimate. If
   this rate is left blank or is less than Borrowing Rate, the
   Borrowing Rate is used to discount salvage value.

CALCULATING THE RESULTS
While entering data, press <RET> without entering a number. Calculation will be performed automatically by the program. The program will return to the TEMPLATE MENU after calculation is complete. IMPORTANT: Do not use the LOTUS <F9> key to calculate.

EXPLANATION OF SUMMARY LEASE VS. PURCHASE INFORMATION
After calculation, a summary block of information titled, "Summary Lease vs. Purchase," is available at the bottom of the template. The information and explanation of it is as follows:
ADV/(DISADV) LEASE - The advantage of leasing versus purchasing is shown for two different present value calculations. The DEBT RATE column shows all cash flows discounted at the debt rate. The RISK ADJ column shows the estimated salvage value discounted at the higher risk-adjusted rate.
AFTER-TAX IRR - The PURCHASE is the pre-tax interest rate times 1 minus the tax rate. The LEASE value is the IRR of the NET CASH FLOW (Line 38).

TECHNICAL INFORMATION AND TEMPLATE LIMITATIONS
The LEASEBUY template can only handle ten time periods. For purposes of the analysis, the useful life of the asset under the purchase alternative is assumed to be equal to the lease term.

PROBLEM
The Lizard Manufacturing Company has decided to acquire a new machine and is trying to determine whether to borrow the required funds from its banker or enter into a financial lease arrangement. Here are the facts:

1. The machine costs $20,000 including installation costs, has a five-year economic life, and an estimated salvage value of $1,000 five years from now.
2. Lizard is able to borrow money from the bank at 11%.
3. If the firm borrows and buys, the asset will be depreciated using the straight-line method.
4. The lease alternative would require the firm to make five equal annual lease payments of $4,500 with the first payment due one year from now. It will be a net lease, which means the firm will have to pay for insurance, maintenance, property taxes, etc. Finally, there is no cancellation option or an option to renew the lease or purchase the asset five years from now.
5. The firm's marginal income tax rate is 30 percent, and management estimates that it will be 30 percent for each of the next five years.
6. Because the salvage value has a higher degree of uncertainty associated with it than the financial flows (debt, lease payments and tax shields), management has decided to utilize a 20% discount rate to discount this cash flow.

From the above information determine:
   a) whether management should lease or purchase the new machine.
   b) what the impact of the higher risk rate for the salvage value has on the decision.

SOLUTION
Choose either the OLD DATA or NEW DATA option and input the information supplied in problem. After entering, the data should appear as follows:

```
======================================
   Purchase Cost           >    20000.0 <
   Annual Lease Payment    >     4500.0 <
   Timing of Payment       >         1 <
   Diff. Operating Cost    >           <
   Term of Lease           >         5 <
   Depreciation Life       >         5 <
   Depreciation Method     >         1 <
   Est. Salvage Val        >     1000.0 <
   Tax Rate                >     30.00%<
   Borrowing Rate          >     11.00%<
   Higher risk rate        >     20.00%<
---------------------------------------
```

After the input data is correct, press <RET> without entering a number and the template will calculate a solution. On a present value basis, with all flows discounted at the after-tax borrowing rate, the lease is $2,010 more favorable than the purchase alternative. Using a higher discount rate on the salvage value causes the present value of the debt purchase to rise, increasing the advantage of the lease by $120 to $2,130. (The rise occurs because the present value is a series of outflows being reduced by the inflow from the salvage value. Valuing the inflow less, raises the present value of the net outflow.)

Choosing either the VIEW or PRINT option will show the results depicted in Exhibit XXV-1 on the next page.

EXHIBIT XXV-1

LEASE-BUY ANALYSIS

===

YEARS:	0	1	2	3	4	5
LEASE:						
Lease Payment	$0	$4,500	$4,500	$4,500	$4,500	$4,500
Tax Saving	$0	$1,350	$1,350	$1,350	$1,350	$1,350
CASH OUTFLOW	$0	$3,150	$3,150	$3,150	$3,150	$3,150
PURCHASE:						
Purchase Outlay	$20,000					
Depreciation		$4,000	$4,000	$4,000	$4,000	$4,000
Oper'ng. Cost		$0	$0	$0	$0	$0
A.T. Salvage		$0	$0	$0	$0	$700
Tax Saving		$1,200	$1,200	$1,200	$1,200	$1,200
CASH OUTFLOW	$20,000	($1,200)	($1,200)	($1,200)	($1,200)	($1,900)
NET CASH FLOW	($20,000)	$4,350	$4,350	$4,350	$4,350	$5,050

===

SUMMARY LEASE VS. PURCHASE

===

DISCOUNTED AT:	DEBT RATE	RISK ADJ *
PV OF LEASE	$12,677	$12,677
PV OF DEBT PURCHASE	$14,688	$14,807 *
ADV/(DISADV) LEASE	$2,010	$2,130

* Salvage after-tax disc. rate 14.00%

AFTER-TAX IRR FOR:
    PURCHASE   7.70%
    LEASE   3.90%

===

PART VIII:
FINANCING

CHAPTER	TOPIC	NAME	PAGE
25	Lease-Buy Analysis	LEASEBUY	149
26	Cost of Capital	COSTCAP	155
27	Leverage	LEVERAGE	157

Part VIII deals with financial decisions. Three models pertain to financing decisions:

LEASEBUY - Model is written up in previous section of the book, Part VII: Capital Budgeting. It is accessible from software from either FINANCING or CAPITAL BUDGETING. Refer to Chapter 25 for the write-up of this model.

COSTCAP - Enables a user to calculate the weighted average cost of capital (WACC) for a company.

LEVERAGE - The purpose of this template is to analyze the effects of operating and financial leverage. Three different capital structures are compared. One is a no-debt capital structure and the others are "low" and "high" debt alternatives as defined by the user.

Chapter 26 COST OF CAPITAL

PURPOSE: The purpose of this template is to calculate the weighted average cost of capital.

LOADING THE TEMPLATE
From the FINANCING sub-menu choose number: 1
From LOTUS choose file name: COSTCAP

TEMPLATE MENU: Menu choices and their functions are as follows:
   DATA - input data
   END - allows the user to leave this template

HOW TO INPUT DATA: Choose DATA option from menu. Cursor will move to the first input field. (Note that input fields are generally shown on the screen between ">" and "<" symbols.) Input for this template is in the range of cells C3 - E9.

EXPLANATION OF CERTAIN INPUTS
Tax Rate - marginal tax rate of the company
Pre-tax Costs/Mkt. Wghts. - Two debt categories and preferred and
   common stock may be used. In cells C6-C9 the pre-tax costs
   (in percentages) are entered. In cells E6-E9 the market
   value of the capital structure component as a percentage of
   the total market value of the company is entered.

   IMPORTANT: The Mkt. Wghts. must equal 100%. If they do not, WACC will calculate as ERR.

CALCULATING THE RESULTS
While entering data, press <RET> without entering a number. Calculation will be performed automatically by the program. The program will return to the TEMPLATE MENU after calculation is complete. IMPORTANT: Do not use the LOTUS <F9> key to calculate.

TECHNICAL INFORMATION AND TEMPLATE LIMITATIONS
The COSTCAP template can only handle two types of debt and one class of preferred and common stock.

PROBLEM
Based on the following information for a firm, compute its weighted average cost of capital.
-- The yield to maturity on outstanding bonds is 13%.
-- The total market value of the bonds is $40 million.
-- There are 5 million common shares outstanding with a market price per share of $25.
-- The required rate of return on the common stock is 14%.
-- The marginal tax rate for the firm is 40%.

SOLUTION

Choose the DATA menu option and input .40 for the tax rate, .13 for the debt and .14 for the equity pre-tax costs. Determine the total market value of the common stock (5 million shares @ $25 per share = $125 million), and add it to the market value of the debt to get a total market value of the firm of $165 million. Then, input the market weights as follows:

```
        debt   - type 40/165 and press <RET>
        common - type 125/165 and press <RET>
```

These entries represent the market weights in percentages. The following is the input that you should have before calculating:

```
              Pre-tax Costs    Mkt. Wghts.
         -------------------------------
         Debt 1    >     13.00%**     24.24%<
         Debt 2    >            **           <
         Preferred>            **           <
         Common    >     14.00%**     75.76%<
         -------------------------------
```

At this point press <RET> without entering a number to calculate the solution. The weighted average cost of capital is 12.50%, and the template solution appears below:

```
         -----------------------------------------------
                  FIRM'S COST OF CAPITAL CALCULATION
                  After-Tax Cost        Wghted Cost
         Debt 1         7.80%               1.89%
         Debt 2         0.00%               0.00%
         Preferred      0.00%               0.00%
         Common        14.00%              10.61%
         WEIGHTED AVERAGE COST OF CAPITAL            12.50%
         ===============================================
```

Chapter 27 LEVERAGE

PURPOSE: The purpose of this template is to analyze the effects of operating and financial leverage. Three different capital structures are compared. One is a no-debt capital structure, and the others are "low" and "high" debt alternatives as defined by the user.

LOADING THE TEMPLATE
From the FINANCING sub-menu choose number: 3
From LOTUS choose file name: LEVERAGE

TEMPLATE MENU
Menu choices available and their functions are as follows:
- DATA - input data
- DATA&HELP - input data with the assistance of the input help screen
- VIEW - view the results of the analysis
- GRAPH - view results in an EPS-EBIT graph
- PRINT - print the results of the analysis
- HELP - view the help screen (shown when template called up)
- END - allows the user to leave this template

HOW TO INPUT DATA
Choose DATA or DATA&HELP option from menu. Cursor will move to the first input field. (Note that input fields are generally shown on the screen between ">" and "<" symbols.) Input for this template is in the range of cells C6 - C19 excluding C9.

EXPLANATION OF CERTAIN INPUTS

Sales $ - the sales level.
Var. Cost % - variable costs as percentage of sales.
Capital $ - the total capital of the company. The total amount of debt, preferred stock and common stock required to support company operations.
Price/Share - the market price per share of common stock.
Preferred % - the percentage of Capital represented by preferred stock.
Pref. Yield - the yield on preferred stock.
Low Debt % - the percentage of Capital represented by debt in the LOW DEBT capital structure.
High Debt % - the percentage of Capital represented by debt in the HIGH DEBT capital structure.
Low Int % - average interest rate on debt in LOW DEBT capital structure.
High Int % - average interest rate on debt in HIGH DEBT capital structure.
Tax Rate % - average corporate tax rate.
Sales Inc. - increment used between sales levels in column E (range E6 to E19) and in EPS-EBIT graph. User may modify this increment to improve the appearance of the graph.

CALCULATING THE RESULTS
While entering data, press <RET> without entering a number. Calculation will be performed automatically by the program. The program will return to the TEMPLATE MENU after calculation is complete. IMPORTANT: Do not use the LOTUS <F9> key to calculate.

TECHNICAL INFORMATION AND TEMPLATE LIMITATIONS
The LEVERAGE template is designed primarily to handle the capital structures of new companies. Three capital structures are investigated at a time. One of these is a no-debt capital structure. Preferred stock may be included in the analysis, but it must represent the same proportion of the capital structure for each of the three capital structures. Different interest rates may be used for different levels of debt, but only one stock price is possible for the three capital structures.

PROBLEM
Mrs. Black is founding a new company to market computers. She projects sales of 100 units the first year at an average selling price of $1,000. Variable costs are expected to be 40% of sales, and fixed operating expenses are expected to be $50,000. Black has determined that she needs $100,000 of capital to start the business and is considering three alternatives:

1. Fund the business with only equity, selling 2,000 shares at $50 each.
2. Sell 1,500 shares at $50 and borrow $25,000 at 12% interest.
3. Sell 1,000 shares at $50 and borrow $50,000 at 15% interest.

The tax rate for the new corporation is expected to average 40% of income. Mrs. Black has asked you to advise her regarding the following issues:

a) the break-even sales required under each of the financing alternatives and the earnings per share (EPS) for each alternative at a sales level of $100,000.
b) the degrees of operating and financial leverage at the $100,000 sales level for all three alternatives.
c) the impact on EPS for each alternative if sales are only $90,000.
d) the "crossover" or "indifference" points with respect to EPS for the financing alternatives.

SOLUTION

Choose the DATA or the DATA&HELP option to input data. Input the information provided. The input will appear as follows:

```
ASSUMPTIONS
************************
Sales $        >  $100,000 <
Var. Cost %    >     40.00%<
Fix. Cost $    >   $50,000 <
------------***********
Capital $      >  $100,000 <
Price/Share    >    $50.00 <
Preferred %    >     0.00%<
Pref. Yield    >     0.00%<
Low Debt %     >    25.00%<
High Debt %    >    50.00%<
Low Int %      >    12.00%<
High Int %     >    15.00%<
Tax Rate %     >    40.00%<
Sales Inc.     >    $2,000 <
---------------------------
```

Note that information pertaining to the Sales Inc. entry was not provided in the problem. This entry is for presentation purposes only and is somewhat arbitrary. The number chosen controls the sales spacing in column E (range E6 - E19) and the X-axis of the graph presentation. Entry choice has no effect on solution values. Choice of a different number would not change your answer to this problem. You may have to experiment with different entries in this category in order to get a satisfactory presentation.

After entering the above input, calculate by pressing <RET> without entering a number. Choosing the VIEW or PRINT option will allow you to view or print the results shown as Exhibit XXVI-1 below.

EXHIBIT XXVI-1

```
================================================================
                                          | EPS FOR DEBT LEVELS:
ASSUMPTIONS              SALES     EBIT   |   NO    LOW    HIGH
************************|----------------|----------------------
Sales $      > $100,000 < 88000   $2,800  $0.84 ($0.08)($2.82)
Var. Cost %  >    40.00%< 90000   $4,000  $1.20   $0.40 ($2.10)
Fix. Cost $  > $50,000 <  92000   $5,200  $1.56   $0.88 ($1.38)
-------------************ 94000   $6,400  $1.92   $1.36 ($0.66)
Capital $    > $100,000 < 96000   $7,600  $2.28   $1.84   $0.06
Price/Share  >    $50.00< 98000   $8,800  $2.64   $2.32   $0.78
Preferred %  >     0.00%< 100000 $10,000  $3.00   $2.80   $1.50
Pref. Yield  >     0.00%< 102000 $11,200  $3.36   $3.28   $2.22
Low Debt %   >    25.00%< 104000 $12,400  $3.72   $3.76   $2.94
High Debt %  >    50.00%< 106000 $13,600  $4.08   $4.24   $3.66
Low Int %    >    12.00%< 108000 $14,800  $4.44   $4.72   $4.38
High Int %   >    15.00%< 110000 $16,000  $4.80   $5.20   $5.10
Tax Rate %   >    40.00%< 112000 $17,200  $5.16   $5.68   $5.82
Sales Inc.   >    $2,000< 114000 $18,400  $5.52   $6.16   $6.54
----------------------------------------------------------------
COMPARATIVE INCOME STATEMENT       NO DEBT  LOW DEBT HIGH DEBT
================================================================
SALES                             $100,000 $100,000 $100,000
VARIABLE COSTS                     $40,000  $40,000  $40,000
FIXED COSTS                        $50,000  $50,000  $50,000
----------------------------------------------------------------
EBIT                               $10,000  $10,000  $10,000
INTEREST                                $0   $3,000   $7,500
TAXES                               $4,000   $2,800   $1,000
----------------------------------------------------------------
NET INCOME                          $6,000   $4,200   $1,500
PREFERRED DIVIDENDS                     $0       $0       $0
AVAILABLE FOR COMMON                $6,000   $4,200   $1,500
----------------------------------------------------------------
EPS                                  $3.00    $2.80    $1.50
================================================================
CAPITAL STRUCTURE:                 NO DEBT LOW DEBT HIGH DEBT
DEBT                                    $0  $25,000  $50,000
PREFERRED                               $0       $0       $0
EQUITY                            $100,000  $75,000  $50,000
SHARES OUTSTANDING                    2000     1500     1000
================================================================
```

(Exhibit continued on next page)

EXHIBIT XXVI-1

(continued from previous page)
===

```
BREAK-EVEN SALES LEVELS:
FOR NET INCOME = 0                 $83,333    $88,333    $95,833
FOR EPS = 0                        $83,333    $88,333    $95,833
=================================================================
DEGREES OF LEVERAGE:
OPERATING LEVERAGE                    6.00       6.00       6.00
FINANCIAL LEVERAGE                    1.00       1.43       4.00
TOTAL LEVERAGE                        6.00       8.57      24.00
=================================================================
EPS INDIFFERENCE POINTS:               EPS      SALES       EBIT
NO DEBT  / LOW DEBT                  $3.60   $103,333    $12,000
NO DEBT  / HIGH DEBT                 $4.50   $108,333    $15,000
LOW DEBT / HIGH DEBT                 $5.40   $110,833    $16,500
=================================================================
```

SELECTED COMMENTS ON SOLUTION

a) Break-even sales for no, low and high debt are $83,333, $88,333 and $95,833 respectively (see Line 44 of template). The EPS for each alternative are $3.00, 2.80 and 1.50 respectively. The EPS are available from either the range of EPS' shown at the top of the template (Line 12) or from the comparative income statement (Line 35).

b) The degrees of operating leverage are 6.00 for all three alternatives. The degrees of financial leverage are 1.00, 1.43 and 4.00 in order of increasing leverage.

c) The impact on EPS for a wide range of sales can be determined from the sales levels shown at the top of the template. For $90,000 in sales, the EPS for each alternative would be $1.20, $0.40 and $(2.10) respectively (Line 7). Alternatively, the user could type 90,000 in the Sales $ input cell (leaving all other inputs as they are), calculate again and then look at line 12 or line 35 as described above in part a).

d) The "crossover" or "indifference" points for EPS are shown at the bottom of the template (Lines 53-55). If EPS were the primary concern, then the No Debt alternative is favorable for sales under $103,333. As sales increase above this point, one of the two debt alternatives yields higher EPS. At sales above $110,833, the high debt alternative yields the highest EPS.

PART IX:
WORKING CAPITAL

CHAPTER	TOPIC	NAME	PAGE
28	EOQ Inventory Model	EOQ	165
29	Cash Balances	CASHBAL	167

Part IX presents two models that deal with working capital management. Both solve for the optimum balances to be held. Balances are deemed to be optimum in the sense that they are cost-minimization balances.

The inventory model (EOQ) is the Economic Order Quantity model. This model determines the amount to order in order to minimize the holding and transactions costs associated with inventory.

The Cash model (CASHBAL) was developed by Baumol via an extension of the EOQ model. It determines the optimum cash balance as that balance which minimizes the sum of opportunity costs (foregone interest income from holding cash) and transactions costs (costs associated with the acquisition or disposition of marketable securities or debt.

Chapter 28 EOQ INVENTORY MODEL

PURPOSE: To determine the economic order quantity and reorder points that will minimize the ordering and holding costs associated with inventory.

LOADING THE TEMPLATE
From the WORKING CAPITAL sub-menu choose number: 1
From LOTUS choose file name: EOQ

TEMPLATE MENU: Menu choices available are as follows:
   DATA - input data
   HELP -
   END - allows the user to leave this template

HOW TO INPUT DATA: Choose DATA menu option. Cursor will move to the first input field. (Note that input fields are generally shown on the screen between ">" and "<" symbols.) Input for this template is in the range of cells D3 - D6.

EXPLANATION OF CERTAIN INPUTS
   Annual Demand - Yearly sales expressed in units
   Ordering Cost - Cost per order
   Holding Cost - Cost associated with holding a unit of
                  inventory
   Lead Time - Time in days between placing an order and
               receiving the order

CALCULATING THE RESULTS
While entering data, press <RET> without entering a number. Calculation will be performed automatically by the program. The program will return to the TEMPLATE MENU after calculation is complete. IMPORTANT: Do not use the LOTUS <F9> key to calculate.

TECHNICAL INFORMATION AND TEMPLATE LIMITATIONS
Model tends to be very simplistic because uniform sales rate and fixed lead time, ordering and holding costs are assumed. Formula used to solve EOQ is as follows:

$$Q = (2SO/c)^{0.5}$$

where
   Q = optimal order size
   S = annual sales per year in units
   O = cost per order
   c = holding cost per unit

PROBLEM:
Part I:

ACME Manufacturing Co. estimates that it will sell 100,000 widgets during the year. If ACME receives immediate service from its supplier, and it costs $100 to place an order and $1.00 per unit in holding costs, answer the following:
- (a) what is the quantity the firm should order to minimize the costs associated with inventory?
- (b) at what point (in terms of units of inventory on hand) should the order be placed?
- (c) what will the average inventory be (in units)?
- (d) what will the total ordering and holding cost be?

Part II:

ACME's supplier has gone bankrupt. Its new supplier requires a lead time of 20 days. Answer (a) - (d) from above.

SOLUTION:
Select the data option, input the information. The screen should look like the following:

```
1  <ALT> B to Restart                ECONOMIC ORDER QUANTITY
2  ================================================================
3  Annual Demand       >    100,000 < Unit sales
4  Ordering Cost       >    $100.00 < Dollars per order
5  Holding Cost        >      $1.00 < Dollars per unit
6  Lead Time           >          0 < Days lead time required for order
7  ----------------------------------------------------------------
8
9  ECONOMIC ORDER QUANTITY           - UNITS              4,472.1
10 REORDER POINT                     - UNITS                  0.0
11 OPTIMAL REORDER TIME              - DAYS                  16.3
12 NUMBER ORDERS PER YEAR            - ORDERS                22.4
13 AVERAGE INVENTORY                 - UNITS              2,236.1
14
15 ANNUAL ORDERING COST                                 $2,236.07
16 ANNUAL HOLDING COST                                  $2,236.07
17                                                      ----------
18 TOTAL ORDERING & HOLDING COST                        $4,472.14
19
20 ================================================================
```

The answers to Part I are as follows:
- (a) 4,472 units
- (b) 0 units (reorder time is instantaneous, so run inventory down to zero before reordering
- (c) 2,236 units
- (d) $4,472 per year

The answers to Part II (screen representation not shown) are the same as Part I except for (b) which is 5,479 units.

Chapter 29 CASH BALANCES

PURPOSE: To determine the optimal quantity of cash balances between cash and marketable securities. This model is based on the work of Baumol who adapted the economic order quantity (EOQ) inventory model to the optimal cash balances decision.

LOADING THE TEMPLATE
From the WORKING CAPITAL sub-menu choose number: 2
From LOTUS choose file name: CASHBAL

TEMPLATE MENU: Menu choices available are as follows:
   DATA - input data
   HELP -
   END - allows the user to leave this template

HOW TO INPUT DATA: Choose DATA menu option. Cursor will move to the first input field. (Note that input fields are generally shown on the screen between ">" and "<" symbols.) Input for this template is in the range of cells D3 - D5.

EXPLANATION OF CERTAIN INPUTS
   Annual Cash - Annual net cash flows for the year
     Transaction Cost - Transaction cost associated with changing the cash position via purchase/sale of marketable securities or borrow/repay debt
     Interest Rate - Interest rate on marketable securities or on borrowings

CALCULATING THE RESULTS
While entering data, press <RET> without entering a number. Calculation will be performed automatically by the program. The program will return to the TEMPLATE MENU after calculation is complete. IMPORTANT: Do not use the LOTUS <F9> key to calculate.

TECHNICAL INFORMATION AND TEMPLATE LIMITATIONS
Model tends to be very simplistic because of the following:
   i.   cash flow is assumed to be uniform over the year.
   ii. transactions costs with either sale/purchase of marketable securities or borrow/repay loan assumed to be equal.
   iii. interest rate for borrowing/lending assumed to be the same.

PROBLEM:
Cashflo, Inc. has a net cash flow of $10,000 per month. If the transaction costs are $100 and the interest rate is 11%, answer the following:
    (a) what is the maximum cash a firm should hold?
    (b) what is the average cash balance?

SOLUTION:
Select data option. Input data from above (remember to convert cash flop from monthly to annual data). The answers are as follows:

    (a) $14,770.98
    (b) $ 7,385.49

The input and solution as it should appear on the screen is shown below:

```
<ALT> B to Restart                 CASH BALANCE (BAUMOL MODEL)
================================================================
Annual Cash          >    $120,000   < Net Annual Cash Flow
Transaction Cost     >    $100.00    < Per Change of Liquidity Position
Interest Rate        >     11.00%    < Lending or Borrowing Rate
----------------------------------------------------------------
                         S O L U T I O N
                ================================================
MAXIMUM CASH BALANCE                                   $14,770.98
AVERAGE CASH BALANCE                                    $7,385.49

REPLENISH CASH (TIME IN DAYS)                               44.9
NUMBER TRANSACTIONS PER YEAR                                 8.1

ANNUAL TRANSACTION COST                                   $812.40
ANNUAL INTEREST COST                                      $812.40
                                                      ------------
TOTAL TRANSACTION & INTEREST COST                       $1,624.81

================================================================
```

NOTES

NOTES